PETER BERRESFORD ELLIS

THE BOYNE
WATER

THE BATTLE OF THE BOYNE, 1690

THE
BLACKSTAFF
PRESS
BELFAST AND ST PAUL, MINNESOTA

First published in 1976 by
Hamish Hamilton Limited
This Blackstaff Press edition is a photolithographic facsimile
of the first edition printed by Western Printing Services, Bristol

This edition published in 1989 by
The Blackstaff Press Limited
3 Galway Park, Dundonald, Belfast BT16 0AN, Northern Ireland
and
Box 5026, 2115 Summit Avenue, St Paul, Minnesota 55105, USA

Printed by The Guernsey Press Company Limited

British Library Cataloguing in Publication Data
Ellis, Peter Berresford, 1943–
The Boyne water: the Battle of the
Boyne, 1690
1. Ireland. Battle of the Boyne
1. Title
941.506
ISBN 0-85640-419-5

Here from my hand as from a cup
  I pour this pure libation;
And ere I drink, I offer up
  One fervant aspiration—
Let man with man, let kin with kin,
  Contend through fields of slaughter—
Whoever fights, may freedom win,
  As then, at the Boyne Water.

> *The Boyne Water*
> *Contemporary Williamite Ballad*

Bitter woe to me are the wounds
  of the land of Fodla,
Who is sorely under a cloud
  whilst her kinsfolk are heartsick.
The trees that were strongest
  in affording their shelter,
Have their branches lopped off
  and their roots withered and decayed.

> *The Wounds of Fodla*
> *Contemporary Jacobite Poem by*
> *Aodhagáin Uí Rathaille*

CONTENTS

Preface   xi

1   Belfast to the Boyne   1

2   July 1, 1690   76

3   The Flight   122

Sources and Acknowledgements   153

Bibliography   154

Index   157

LIST OF ILLUSTRATIONS

Between pages 36 *and* 37

1. William III.
   Portrait after W. Wissing

1b. James II.
   Portrait by G. Kneller, 1684–5

2a. Friedrich Herman, first duke of Schomberg, William's Captain-General at the Boyne

2b. Richard Talbot, earl and titular duke of Tyrconnell, James II's Captain-General at the Boyne.
   French school, 1690

3a. Prince George of Daamstadt.
   Portrait by M. Dahl, 1705

3b. Hans Willem Bentinck, afterwards 1st earl of Portland, who wrote the official Williamite account of the battle.
   Studio of H. Rigaud

4a. Godart, Baron Ginkel, Dutch cavalry commander at the Boyne who afterwards became William's commander-in-chief.
   Mezzotint by I. Smith

4b. James Butler, second duke of Ormonde, commander of William's English Horse Guards at the battle.
   Attributed to M. Dahl, 1714

Between pages 68 *and* 69

5. Jacobites defending the crossings into Oldbridge across the Boyne.
   From a modern print by Cecil C. P. Lawson, *c.* 1930

6. The river Boyne at the point of William's main crossing at Oldbridge. The hill of Donore is to the left of the picture and the site of the Jacobite artillery is just behind the house on the left.

7a. Williamite troops gaining a foothold in Oldbridge.
An etching by R. de Hodge, published by Allard Carolus, 1690

7b. Williamite artillery firing towards the Boyne with Oldbridge to the right.
From an engraving by Theodor Mass.

Between pages 124 *and* 125

8. William attempting to lead the Dutch cavalry across the Boyne.
Aquatint by J. Grozer after B. West, 1771

9. William III entering Dublin on Sunday, 6 July, 1690.
A contemporary etching published by A. Schoonebeek, 1690

10. The River Boyne at Rosnaree, at the spot where Count Meinhard Schomberg began his feint attack, crossing with a division of 10,000 men and opposed by Sir Neil O'Neil's 480 dragoons

11. Patrick Sarsfield, Major-General of cavalry for James at the Boyne.
Engraving by M. A. Bregeon

Illustrations 1a, 1b, 2b, 3a, 3b, 4b, are reproduced by kind permission of the National Portrait Gallery, London; illustrations 2a, 4a, 5, 7a, 8, 9 are reproduced by kind permission of the National Army Museum, London; illustration 11 is reproduced by kind permission of the National Gallery of Ireland; illustration 7b is reproduced by kind permission of the National Library of Ireland; and illustrations 6 and 10 by kind permission of Bord Failte Eireann.

Maps drawn by Patrick Leeson

Ireland 1690   *page* 2
The Battle of the Boyne   *pages* 100–101

PREFACE

This is not another chronicle of the Jacobite War in Ireland of 1689–91. It is the story of one particular battle which has become a political symbol in Ireland; a battle fought across the River Boyne on July 1, 1690. No other battle in history has created the effect that the Battle of the Boyne has and yet, in terms of the war itself, it was not of great military significance. Although it resulted in a defeat for the Jacobite forces and precipitated the flight of James II to France, the Jacobite losses were not great and the main bulk of these forces retreated in good order, re-grouped before Limerick, and held out against the Williamites for another twelve months.

In terms of military significance, the Battle of Aughrim was the decisive conflict of the war. So tremendous was the disaster from the Jacobite viewpoint and, because of their wholehearted support for the cause, the Irish viewpoint, that it was one hundred years before an Irish army took the field again when Jacobinism had replaced Jacobitism as the rallying philosophy of the Irish nation, uniting as it did Catholic, Protestant and Dissenter.

Why, then, did the Boyne and not Aughrim 'of the slaughter' —as the poet Seámas Dall Mac Cuarta called it—capture the imagination?

No battle has left such an indelible impression on the folk memory of the Irish people. Each year members of the Protestant religion in the north of Ireland celebrate the Williamite victory with parades. The songs, poems, pipe music and dances that recall the event are too numerous to mention. Yet while invocations are made to the event, the event as an historical incident is obscured and has been for many years in the name of political expediency.

The Battle of the Boyne is still celebrated as the day 'when William of Orange, and our immortal forefathers, overthrew the Pope and Popery at the Boyne. Then began the era of civil and religious liberty'. That myth, that the mainly Presbyterian colonists in Ireland achieved an 'era of civil and religious liberty' from Catholic oppression that 'excessive hot day' of July 1, 1690, at the Boyne, is one I hope the following narration will clarify.

PETER BERRESFORD ELLIS

CHAPTER I

BELFAST TO THE BOYNE

'a battle is hardly to be avoided'

The cannons ceased to fire at eight o'clock in the evening. Ever since three o'clock in the afternoon, the four six-pounder field guns, supported by four squat howitzers, manned by the sweating gunners of the army of William Henry of Orange, William III of England by popular acclaim, had poured shot across the river which separated them from the army of William's father-in-law, the deposed James II. The battery had been placed a hundred yards away from the banks of the River Boyne, on a level section of the undulating ground which faced the Jacobite positions on the far side of the river, centred round the few stone houses and the ugly squat towered church which comprised the little hamlet of Oldbridge. To the east of the hamlet, immediately south of the Williamite positions, a battery of six Jacobite six-pounders had been engaging all afternoon in a fierce artillery duel. A few men and horses had been killed but otherwise the Jacobite gunnery was not very accurate, while the Williamite guns had managed to destroy two guns in the Jacobite battery, killing and disabling their crews.

It had, according to Colonel Sir Thomas Bellingham, an aide-de-camp on William's general staff, been a very hot day and the gunners were sweat-soaked, grimy and exhausted after five hours of almost continual firing. The six foot long iron barrels of the cannons were too hot to touch and the gun captains had long since decreased the number of shots from the maximum fifteen per hour to well under ten per hour. One Williamite soldier estimated that the opposing Jacobite battery had fired only an average of seven shots per hour per cannon, but it was known that the Jacobites had little in the way of artillery and even less in the way of ammunition and supplies for it. The four Williamite cannons, however, represented only a fraction of William's main artillery train, consisting of some

fifty pieces, including massive twenty-four-pounders, which were still at the rear of the lines.

The gun smoke hung low and thick over the river, almost obscuring both armies from each other. The last salvo of the day was fired by the Williamite guns. As with each salvo, the gunners carefully ladled a pound and a half of powder into the six foot long iron barrel; an assistant gunner stepped briskly forward with a long wooden plunger, and rammed the powder down the barrel. Then the six pound iron shot was placed into the barrel and similarly rammed home. Each gunner then placed a small pinch of powder in the touch hole. The gun captains crouched behind the guns, sighting on the enemy's position with a quadrant, making sure each gun was accurately pointed towards a fairly good target, before stepping clear. The gunners stood ready with lighted linstocks. On the shouted order 'fire!', the linstocks came down on the touch hole and the cannons roared, bouncing back several yards on their massive iron rimmed wheels. The last shots fell harmlessly round the Jacobite gun battery, the Williamite officers noting the fall of each shot through their field glasses.

It was as if by mutual consent that both the Jacobite and Williamite guns fired no more, each crew securing their guns for the night, knowing that the heavy artillery duel of the day was but a prelude to what was about to take place on the morning. But tomorrow was a lifetime away. Now the gunners could bathe their tired limbs in the stream that gurgled down one of the deep gorges towards the Oldbridge ford, eat a meal and retire to their tents for the night.

Most of the army had bedded down at nightfall, about ten o'clock that evening of June 30, 1690. The majority had needed little urging because they had been roused at two o'clock that morning to commence their march to this spot and it was more than likely that the officers would be rousing them at an unearthly hour. And they realised that the next day a battle would have to be fought. But few men except the generals, now gathered in William's headquarters in the grey stone former Cistercian abbey of Mellifont, two miles to the north-west of Oldbridge, paid much heed to the forthcoming battle. Few soldiers of William's army doubted the outcome; after all, they outnumbered the tattered Jacobite army, they had nearly five times the artillery that James had, and they were better fed, armed and supplied. But, above all, the soldiers of William had a simple belief that God was on their side. No, such worries were not for William's soldiers that night. There were more important problems to be considered, where to pitch their tents, where to get straw and extra blankets, and where each regimental wagon was with the brandy rations to which each man was entitled before the start of the battle. The straw and extra blankets were, perhaps, the most important concern for, in spite of the 'excessive hot days' of the summer, as Bellingham called them, the nights were extremely chilly, causing thick mists to rise and lay close to the ground for several hours before the sun dispersed them and warmed the shivering, yawning, grumbling men.

Some 35,000 Williamite troops now lay encamped among the small hills along the northern bank of the Boyne river from Tullyeskar, just north of Drogheda, to Tullyallen and Townley Hall. They were a mixture of many nationalities; there were Dutch, Danes, French, German, English, English and Scottish settlers from many parts of Ireland, Swiss, Italians, Norwegians and Poles. All of them had given their allegiance to William of Orange and the League of Augsburg. The English saw themselves fighting for the new King of England against the despotic old King who had so usurped the power entrusted to him that they had been forced to depose him. The colonists in Ireland saw William as the monarch who would save them from the native Irish, risen to reclaim the lands from which they had been driven by English conquest and confiscation. The other nationalities saw William as the representative of the Grand Alliance formed to stop Louis XIV of France in his attempt to conquer and dominate Europe. Louis was supporting his ally James in his efforts to regain the throne of England.

The 25,000 men of the Jacobite army were likewise a mixed force of English, Irish, French, German and Dutch. But these men had not the certainty of victory of the Williamites; not even their Captain-General, the sixty-year-old Duke of Tyrconnell, held out the hope of a Jacobite success. He had vainly advised James not to fight this battle but to march his army westward along the Boyne valley, avoiding all conflict with the enemy for as long as possible. It was advice echoed by M. le Comte de Lauzun, the commander of the French division and Louis XIV's newly appointed adviser to James. But James had decided to ignore their advice, for if he did not make an attempt to stop William at the Boyne Dublin would fall into the hands of the enemy and, with Dublin gone, most of Ireland would also fall. James felt he would be forced back into the province of Connaught without supplies and, if that happened, it would be merely a question of time before the Jacobites tasted defeat. Another important consideration was the fear that the morale of his army would crumble if he kept retreating before William. Already the soldiers were grumbling because during the past week they had retreated before William's advance from Dundalk to Ardee and from Ardee to the Boyne. Many of James' younger general officers, like his own son (the Duke of Berwick) and Major-General Patrick Sarsfield, had censured him for not standing against the Williamites in Moyry Pass, just north of Dundalk, which observers on both sides agreed was an ideal site where a thousand Jacobites could have held up William's entire army for months. Over-riding the advice of his experienced military advisers, James decided that the time to make a stand against William was now. He observed in his *Memoirs* that if a battle was to be risked 'there was not any situation more favourable; and if he continued always retreating, he would have lost all without striking a stroke, and have been driven fairly into the sea'. Unwillingly Tyrconnell and Lauzun had resigned themselves to battle. Lauzun had written: 'And so in spite of all our care a battle is hardly to be avoided.' But, he added, 'I will, however, do all possible not to let it come to a decisive battle for I see beforehand the consequences.'

'*My own children have forsaken me*'

For one of two men, James Stuart and William Henry Nassau, July 1, 1690, would mean the end of their dynasty. The road to the Boyne had begun when James II succeeded his brother Charles to the throne in February 1685, at the age of fifty-two. He was a man who had physical courage, sincerity, tenacity and industry but he had little understanding of his fellow men and would misjudge every situation. He lacked diversity of mind and had little sense of humour. James, like his brother, was a Catholic but, unlike his brother, was openly and aggressively

so. At first, on his accession in February 1685, he had pro-
claimed his pledge to protect the Protestant Anglican Church. A
few months after his succession an attempted uprising by the
Scottish Protestants in an effort to depose him or at least wrest
Scotland from the rule of a Catholic king, had rallied the entire
country behind James. Then came Monmouth's uprising which
was firmly suppressed at the battle of Sedgemoor and punished
by the 'Bloody Assizes' held under the auspices of Judge
Jeffreys. Three hundred and fifty supporters of Monmouth
were executed and a further eight hundred sold into slavery in
the colonies. The ruthlessness of the suppression shocked the
people of England. Even John Churchill, the general whose
energy had made Sedgemoor a victory for James, struck at a
mantelpiece and commented: 'This marble is not harder than
the King's heart!'

James used the uprising as a pretext to establish a very large
standing army. Parliament was horrified when James decided
to by-pass them, holding them in abeyance while he used his
dispensing power to appoint Catholics into key positions in the
kingdom. He told Parliament in 1686 that whether legal or not
they could not question his appointment of Catholic officers to
the army. Parliament demanded the recall of the illegal commissions and even the House of Lords took a firm stand against
the King. James prorogued both houses and, as the situation
worsened, dissolved them altogether. He now had no check on
his impulsive actions and started to dismiss High Court judges
and replace them with Catholics and even appoint Catholics to
his Privy Council.

It became obvious that James was seeking to return Protestant England, Wales and Scotland to the Catholic fold and to
establish an absolute monarchy of the type Louis XIV enjoyed
in France. To do this James needed Louis' gold and Louis'
soldiers. France had emerged as the dominant power in Europe
at the expense of Spain and Austria and, at first, England had
concluded a triple alliance against her with Holland and
Sweden. But Charles II, who had conducted the alliance, had
put it to Louis that his Parliament would grant him ample
funds to oppose the French militarily—how much, he asked,
was Louis prepared to pay him not to? A secret treaty—the
Treaty of Dover—had been concluded bringing England into
opposition with Holland.

This secret treaty was now viewed with increasing alarm in England as a threat to the English constitution and, in particular, the Established Church. Europe was already trembling at the powerful military ambitions of Louis XIV and was now fearful of his increasing religious bigotry. In 1686 Louis revoked the Edict of Nantes by which Henri IV, having abandoned the Protestant faith in favour of Catholicism, had decreed toleration and free exercise of their faith to his Protestant subjects. Now a hundred thousand French Protestants were forced to flee from France to Holland, Switzerland, the Palatinate and England. Many Huguenots settled in Ireland, particularly in the area around Lisburn. This act of Louis was uppermost in the minds of most Englishmen when James began to reorganise the army, appoint Catholic officers and open Catholic Churches. Carmelites, Benedictines and Franciscans appeared openly in their habits in London for the first time for many years and the Jesuits set up a school in central London. Henry VIII and Elizabeth I had used their 'ecclesiastical supremacy' as a weapon by which to change the Church of England from Catholic to Protestant. James was now determined to use that same 'supremacy' to reverse matters.

The majority of English Catholic gentry stood aloof from James' activities and predicted the inevitable consequences of his folly. To those who opposed his sectarian revolution James would stamp his feet and declare: 'I am King! I will be obeyed!' In 1687 James tried to split the Protestant opposition by the Declaration of Indulgence which annulled the penal laws against Nonconformists and Catholics alike. But Protestant dissenters, led by the example of people such as John Bunyan, refused to accept the Indulgence.

During the summer of 1688 England had stood on the brink of civil war. Seven Anglican bishops led by the primate Archbishop William Sancroft had protested against the use of James' dispensing powers. Enraged, James said, 'It is a standard of rebellion' and ordered them to be tried for seditious libel. Demonstrations were made in their favour and at their trial on June 29 they were declared 'Not Guilty'. Joyous demonstrations shook the kingdom. That night, as the demonstrations, fireworks and cannon roars greeted their release, some men sat down and wrote a letter to William Henry Nassau, Prince of Orange, and husband to James' eldest daughter Mary. They were the lords Shrewsbury, Danby, Russell, Bishop Compton, Devonshire, Lumley and Henry Sidney. The basis of the suggestion, carried in their letter, was that William should come to England and depose his despotic father-in-law.

Throughout the tumults of the last few years the political leaders in England had thought that James would be succeeded by his daughter Mary. Her husband William, Prince of Orange, had been called to head the Hollandish Republic following the fall of John de Witt after the army of Louis XIV invaded Holland in 1672. In spite of his weak constitution—he was a constant sufferer of asthma—the young twenty-two-year-old Stadholder managed to win back province after province from the veteran French general the Prince de Condé. Over the years William had managed to form an alliance with various Catholic and Protestant countries to check the ambitions of France. He had, however, thrown his support in favour of James II in order to secure the succession for his wife. But now William was confronted with a problem—late in their life James and his wife, Mary of Modena, had been blessed by the birth of a son, born on June 10 of that year of 1688, James, Prince of Wales. It was with foreboding for the future that Protestant England noted that his godfather was the Papal Nuncio d'Adda and that he was to be brought up in the Catholic faith. Rumours were even spread that the child was not James' but a trick to prevent his daughter's succession.

With the arrival of the letter from England, William decided to act and accepted the invitation on his and his wife's behalf. On November 5, 1688, William landed at Torbay. James was not worried. After all, he had an army of 40,000 men and he expected his ally, Louis, to throw his armies against his old enemy Holland which would mean the immediate recall of William. But Louis, in what was to be the greatest political error of his reign, threw his forces against Germany. Thus secure, the States-General of Holland gave their sanction to William's adventure. James now found himself deserted on all sides for even his generals, like Lord John Churchill, went over to William. The last straw came when his second daughter Anne left him to join the Williamites at Nottingham. 'God help me!' cried a dejected James, now utterly broken in spirit, 'for my own children have forsaken me!' On the night of December 11 James, completely deserted, tried to escape from London but was captured. A few days later he managed another, this time successful, attempt and succeeded in reaching St. Germain in France where his wife and their baby son had already established themselves.

Under the guidance of the leaders of the revolution William called a Convention Parliament. A section of the Tory Party, led by the Earl of Clarendon, Mary's uncle, suggested that James remain titular King but that William should act as Regent. Others felt that Mary should now become Queen in her own right. The whole matter hinged on William who was not going to be content with the mere title of honorary consort. After protracted debates, in which the proposal for the Regency was lost by only a single vote (and William had told Lord Danby he had no wish to be his wife's gentleman-usher), it was decided to make William and Mary joint monarchs. On February 13, 1689, the Convention Parliament presented a Declaration of Rights to William and Mary, reciting James' misgovernment and the resolve of Parliament to assert the ancient rights and liberties of English subjects. It denied the right of any king to exercise a dispensing power, to exact money or to maintain an army save by consent of Parliament. It asserted for the subject a right of petition, a free choice of representation in Parliament, liberty for Parliament to debate and the impartial administration of justice. In full faith that these principles were accepted by them, it declared William and Mary were now King and Queen of England. William's fear that the Whig Party policies would lead to a reconstitution of the old Commonwealth republic caused him to immediately dissolve the Convention Parliament with 'its work all unfinished' and hold new elections, ensuring that in the next Parliament a Tory domination was secured.

In France Louis XIV's moves against Germany had been met with a stubborn resistance. The outrages of the French army had forced a Grand Alliance to be set up at Augsburg. This alliance was formed by both Protestant and Catholic rulers who were determined to prevent the political and military ambitions of Louis for the domination of Europe from being realised. Among the leaders of the Grand Alliance was Benedetto Odescalchi, Pope Innocent XI, who had quarrelled violently with Louis. At first he had disagreed vehemently with Louis' revocation of the Edict of Nantes, considering it a worthless act of folly. The subsequent French bombardment of Genoa, and Louis' march on Rome itself, had caused Innocent XI to be an enthusiastic supporter of the Augsburg alliance.

Now that William was head of state in England Louis XIV saw that England had become a very important pawn in his European chess game. If he could re-establish James as head of state it would not only destroy the threat England now posed but would, if the plan succeeded, create a strong ally against the Grand Alliance. But in England not a sword had been raised in defence of James II. How could James set out to regain the throne in what was to all appearances a totally hostile country? A weak point would have to be found. That weak point was Ireland.

Since the Cromwellian land settlement, which had been confirmed at the Restoration of the Stuart monarchy, the problem in Ireland had ceased to be one of Gaelic separatism but one of land and religion. Cromwell's policy had treated all Catholic landowners alike, whether they were Irish or the Old English colonists who had settled in Ireland at various times prior to 1600. During the closing months of the Commonwealth administration the Old English colonists in Ireland had declared for Charles II together with most of the mainly Presbyterian settlers of Ulster, who had colonised the province during the first half of the century. But the colonists who had flocked to Ireland during the Cromwellian period were mainly republican or protectorate supporters and it was only after a firm assurance from Charles on the question of land settlement that they felt disposed towards a Stuart Restoration. The Old English Catholics, deprived of their land by the Commonwealth settlers, looked forward to having their estates returned to them at the Restoration. In turn, the native Irish, dispossessed by both Old English and Commonwealth colonists, supported the Stuarts in the belief that their lands would also be returned. When the event did come about, the Restoration was a result of the Commonwealth army's support and the maintenance of the Cromwellian land settlement in Ireland was a necessary concession that Charles readily agreed to as part of the bargain. Charles did return the estates to some of his favourites but for the most part the Cromwellian colonists remained secure.

Charles had actually stated in 1660 that the Irish and Old English landowners would have their estates returned and, in the same statement, that the Cromwellian colonists would be able to keep what they had. The first Duke of Ormonde, then Lord-Lieutenant of Ireland, dryly commented that a new, larger Ireland would have to be found to meet the promise. The land question dominated the Irish political scene during the twenty-five years of Charles II's reign, a reign that was basically one of peace and a comparative prosperity, with the new Cromwellian colonists owning nearly all of Ulster, half of Connaught, and four-fifths of Leinster and Munster. The position of the Catholic Church ranged from toleration and semi-official recognition immediately after the Restoration to bitter persecution during the last years of Charles' life. This persecution was brought about in the aftermath of the 'Popish Plot' hysteria from England. The Catholic clergy were driven underground and church leaders, such as Archbishop Oliver Plunkett, were executed. In spite of the religious conflict and commercial restrictions imposed by England, Ireland thrived as a commercial entity. Butter exports to Europe, salt beef to America, sheep rearing, the Ulster-centred linen industry and fish exports all helped to contribute to a growth in the wealth of the new colonists. It should be noted, too, that workers were only paid half the wages paid in England. This prosperity drew more and more colonists to the country and 80,000 Presbyterian Scots were listed as arriving in the year 1672 alone.

The land settlement was one of the essential planks of English imperial rule in Ireland and James was, naturally enough, also committed to maintaining that rule. His new Lord-Lieutenant, Lord Clarendon, made it clear: 'I have the King's commands to declare upon all occasions that, whatever imaginary . . . apprehensions any men may have had, His Majesty has no intention of altering the Acts of Settlement.' But the Irish and Old English let James' Catholicism blind them to his imperialism and they had now become firmly Jacobite and felt that James was just playing politics. According to Colonel Charles O'Kelly, 'the Irish exulted in the assured hope that their sovereign . . . would forthwith restore to the heavenly powers their temples and altars and also to the natives their properties and estates of which they had been for so many years unjustly despoiled'.

Richard Talbot became leader of the Old English Catholic faction. He had been created Earl of Tyrconnell in 1685 and he

promptly set about securing a recognition of the Catholic
Church in Ireland and began to carry out the Catholicisation
of the army. In January 1687, Tyrconnell was created Lord
Deputy. The general feeling of the colonists was encapsulated
in a satirical ballad composed by the then thirty-nine-year-old
Whig politician, Thomas Wharton, who described the mutual
congratulations of a couple of Irishmen upon the coming
triumph of Catholicism and the old landowners in Ireland. At
first the verses attracted little attention until someone set them
to some music composed by Daniel Purcell, the brother of
Henry, as a harpsichord exercise. Within a few weeks it was
being sung all over the kingdoms of Ireland, England and
Scotland. The song was called *Lillebulero*:

> Ho brother Teig dost hear the decree
> Lillebulero bullen a la
> Dat we shall have a new deputy
> Lillebulero bullen a la
> Le ro le ro le ro le
> Lillebulero bullen a la
> Lillebulero le ro le ro
> Lillebulero bullen a la
>
> Ho, by my soul, it is a Talbot
> Lillebulero bullen a la
> And he will cut all de English throat
> Lillebulero bullen a la
> Le ro le ro le ro le
> Lillebulero bullen a la
> Lillebulero le ro le ro
> Lillebulero bullen a la.

The 'nonsense' line is said to have come from the Irish phrase
an lile ba léir é, ba linn an lá—the lily was triumphant, we won
the day.

The Old English and the Irish were enthusiastic at the new
move. Dermot MacCarthy of Munster thought he saw the
prospect of freedom for the Irish nation.

> Behold there the Gaels in arms, every one of them,
> They have powder and guns, hold the castles and fortresses;
> The Presbyterians, lo, have been overthrown,
> And the fanatics have left an infernal smell after them.
> Whither shall John turn? He has now no red coat on him,
> Nor 'Who's there?' on his lips when standing beside the gate.
> 'You Popish rogue' they won't dare to say to us,
> But 'Cromwellian dog' is the watchword we have for him.

A fellow Munster poet, Daithi Ó Bruadair, who had sadly watched and written bitterly during the black years of Cromwellian persecution, was also heartened at the new state of affairs. In a poem *Caithréim Theidhg*, The Triumph of Teig, he wrote:

> The thing that has wounded John sorely, and others too,
> Is that Tadhg from the mountain should rise to so high a rank
> That *Cia Sud** should be thinking of nothing but revelry
> And Who's There should now be a plundered old driveller.
> After Raif's† conduct, his prating and swaggering
> His sword and his pike, lo, are they not held by Flaherty?

Ireland was now firmly Jacobite. The Old English saw their support of James as a way of getting back their estates from the newer Cromwellian colonists while the native Irish landowners, dispossessed steadily during the last 150 years, also saw their support leading to a similar achievement. For the majority of landless Irish, the old ideal of freedom from the alien conqueror was played upon. The overthrow of James II in England had therefore created a great deal of confusion in the country. A dangerous situation looked like developing and rumours flew among the colonists that the Irish, aided by the Old English, would rise up, as they had done in 1641, and massacre them. December 9, 1688, was said to be the day of the insurrection and this caused thousands of frightened settlers to flee to England. Dean William King of St. Patrick's, Dublin, noted in his diary that each day ships left 'laden mostly with women, children and such goods as they could get on board'. The colonists in the north declared their support for William and Mary and those in Derry shut their gates on the regiment of Lord Antrim, sent there to investigate reports that the Derry citizens had been making overtures to William.

The Lord Deputy, Tyrconnell, did his best to pacify the fears of the colonists, causing the Archbishop of Dublin to have a reassuring message read in all Anglican churches and making several proclamations promising protection to those colonists who remained loyal to James. Tyrconnell had at first entered into communication with William. Richard Hamilton, one of the well-known Catholic Hamilton brothers and nephew of the first Duke of Ormonde, was sent to Ireland to negotiate but on

---

* Who's There, challenge of English soldiers.
† Raif = Ralph, Irish name for an Englishman.

reaching Dublin he joined Tyrconnell and urged him to remain loyal to James. Tyrconnell was, by March 1689, in firm control of all Ireland with the exception of enclaves in Sligo, Derry, Enniskillen and some other colonist settlements in the province of Ulster. He had ignored William's command of February 22, 1689, to lay down his arms and submit to him.

For Louis XIV's strategy, therefore, the weak point was Ireland. It was through Ireland that James would return to the throne of England. On February 15, 1689, James left St. Germain and on March 12 he arrived at the port of Kinsale in Co. Cork, the first English monarch to set foot in Ireland for three centuries. With James came a considerable reinforcement of soldiers, officers and arms. The Stuart monarch entered Dublin on Palm Sunday, March 24, to universal acclaim.

Ireland was Jacobite but the Jacobites had underestimated the determination of the colonists in Derry and Enniskillen to hold out against James. While the Jacobite army dithered over the storming of these strongpoints, James summoned a Parliament to meet in May to carry out 'liberty of conscience' and to 'the relieving of such as have been injured by the late acts of settlement, as far as may be consistent with reason, justice and the public good of my people'. The old ideals of the Confederate Parliament of an independent state sharing a monarchy with England seemed about to be realised. The people reckoned without James. The members of the Irish Parliament introduced a bill to repeal Poynings' Law so that 'the Irish Parliament will be made independent of England'. The bill was dropped under pressure from James although he did, with great reluctance, agree to an act declaring that the English parliament had no right to legislate for Ireland. James certainly did not like any idea of separation from England and, as he himself had written, he felt the provisions of the act were 'such diminutions of his prerogative as nothing but his unwillingness to disgust those who were otherwise affectionate subjects could have exhorted from him'.

The Irish Parliament pressed on with its legislation and passed acts which made all religions equal under the law and ordered that each sect should support their own priests or ministers. But the primary object of the Parliament was the repeal of the Cromwellian land settlement. James' English advisers strongly opposed this and James threatened to dissolve the parliament. The Old English and the Irish threatened to take no further part in supporting James with military aid and the Stuart monarch's French advisers pointed out that it was in his interest not to oppose the bill *in toto*. Finally James had to give his very reluctant assent to the bill which stated that the acts of settlement were invalid and that the landowners of 1641, or their heirs, were authorised to take steps to recover their property. All outlawries arising from the insurrection were cancelled.

The workings of the Jacobite Irish Parliament in Dublin had done considerable damage to James' reputation among his Irish subjects. It had been clearly demonstrated that James viewed Ireland as the stepping stone to England, indeed, as Louis XIV intended it should be, and that James was reluctant to make any concessions to the Irish that would alienate him from English public opinion. His keeping the Irish Parliament under English control, his refusal to allow the repeal of Poynings' Law, and his attempted blocking of the repeal of the acts of settlement, demonstrated that James would not undo the English conquest of the country but merely re-establish the Old English conquerors over the new English colonists and both would still be masters to the native Irish. Nevertheless, the majority still gave their support to James because the alternative, if the new English colonists continued in dominance, was an infinitely worse prospect.

Thus dependent on the battle about to be fought on July 1, 1690, was not only the fate of two royal dynasties, not just a fight for the strategic advancement of Louis XIV of France in his plans to dominate Europe, but the prospect for the Irish people of yet another reconquest, yet another land settlement, followed by confiscations and new colonists settling in the country and, possibly, the eventual extinction of the Irish nation.

'Never were people more welcome'

On June 14, 1690, William arrived in Belfast Lough. He had set sail from Hoylake, Lancashire, at noon on June 11 in a fleet consisting of six men-o'-war commanded by a flamboyant

officer called Sir Cloudesley Shovell, Rear-Admiral of the Blue.
Shovell had been knighted for his part in a sea battle off Bantry
Bay during the previous year when Admiral Arthur Herbert's
fleet had fought an action with the French. Both sides had
claimed a victory. Earlier in the year Shovell had raided several
Jacobite harbours in Ireland including an almost sensational
attack on Dublin when he captured and took out of Dublin
harbour a twenty gun Jacobite frigate, an event reported with
great glee in the *London Gazette* on April 28. Under the protection
of Sir Cloudesley's warships were six yachts and other vessels. On
board the royal yacht *Mary*, commanded by Sir Grenville
Collins, was William, while Prince Georg of Daamstadt, the
portly husband of Mary's sister Anne, was on board the
Henrietta, commanded by Captain Sanderson.

William was well aware that Ireland was now the corner
stone for the campaign in Europe. He believed that the Irish
campaign would drag on unless he went there himself and provided the necessary dash and inspiration he felt that his present
commander-in-chief, the veteran Duke of Schomberg, lacked.
Hearing that the colonists in Ulster had declared for him and
were holding out in Derry and Enniskillen against besieging
Jacobite forces, William had despatched the forty-three-year-
old Major-General Percy Kirk to relieve Derry in May 1689.
Kirk had arrived with four men-o'-war, twenty-six transports
and store ships in mid June but it was not until July 27, after
105 days, that the siege was raised. A few days later the battle
of Newtownbutler was fought and won by the Williamites,
relieving the pressure on Enniskillen. But still large tracts of
Ulster were in Jacobite hands. To finish the job William had
sent the Duke of Schomberg.

Friedrich Herman, Duke of Schomberg, was born in Heidel-
berg in December 1615, the son of Hans Meinhard von
Schönberg (later spelled Schomberg) and Anne, daughter of
Edward Sutton, the ninth Lord Dudley. He had a distinguished
career in the army of Louis XIV but on the revocation of the
Edict of Nantes he had joined the Elector of Brandenburg's
army which then became part of the Grand Alliance. He had
followed William to England and had joined a committee for
Irish Affairs whose main task was to raise new regiments to
fight in Ireland. In March 1689, the House of Commons had
voted funds to equip an army of 20,000 men and supply it for a

six month period. It took several months to organise the army, mainly due to the neglect of the Commissary-General John Shales who, it was rumoured, was sympathetic to the Irish Jacobites. The arms and provisions were so sub-standard that it was alleged he had been bribed to authorise their purchase. Schomberg was officially appointed to the Irish command in mid July and he sailed from Hoylake on August 12 with twelve regiments of foot, leaving his horse and the rest of the army to follow as soon as they were ready. Schomberg landed at Belfast Lough the following day where they were met by some colonists who fell 'on their knees with tears in their eyes and thanking God and the English for their deliverance, telling the soldiers never were people more welcome, kissing them for joy', or so said the contemporary news-sheet *Great news from the army*.

The Jacobites had not opposed Schomberg's landing although they were in control of the area. Two Jacobite regiments were stationed in Carrickfergus Castle while Major-General Thomas Maxwell had a force of horse and dragoons in the Belfast area which could have disputed the infantry landings. Indeed, Schomberg had expected such an attack, remarking 'if they have one dram of courage or wit they will attack us this night since they will never expect the like opportunity'. Surprisingly, Maxwell retreated and by early September Schomberg had landed nearly 20,000 men although, according to the *London Gazette* of September 12, 1689, the figure was boosted to 30,000. There were now nineteen foot regiments, including three Huguenot regiments, as well as two regiments of William's crack Dutch troops, plus six cavalry regiments and a dragoon regiment. In addition to this, included on the Williamite army musters, were the recently raised colonial regiments of Derry and Enniskillen. Now, in overwhelming numbers, Schomberg attacked Carrickfergus, held against him by Cormac O'Neill and MacCarthy Mor. After a week of spirited defence the Jacobites made terms but one of Schomberg's officers admitted that they were 'not too strictly observed by us'. George Warter Story, serving as a chaplain with one of the Williamite regiments, blamed the colonists for ill-treating the Jacobites, even stripping women and forcing them to run the gauntlet. Schomberg, according to Story, had ridden, pistol in hand, among the colonists to try to prevent the Jacobites from being murdered.

At this time Marshal Conrad von Rosen, James' military adviser from Louis XIV, estimated that the Jacobite army could put only six to seven thousand troops into the field of which a third were unarmed. It was felt that Schomberg would now seize this advantage and, with the principal areas of Ulster secured, march straight for Dublin which, the Jacobite generals informed James, was untenable. They advised him to march his army across the river Shannon and hold out in Connaught until French reinforcements could be landed. James ignored their advice and showed some of the courage and dash that had won him a reputation at the Battle of the Dunes. He 'resolved not to be tamely walked out of Ireland but to strike one blow for it at least'. With Tyrconnell's support he set off for Drogheda with a small force of two hundred guards and volunteers, reaching it on August 26. He ordered his son Berwick to conduct a delaying action around Newry, breaking up causeways, bridges and holing roads, while he organised the training of a force to meet Schomberg.

Schomberg left Belfast on September 2, reaching Newry on the 5th but Berwick had completed his harassing action and Schomberg's troops were soon in difficulty. As Story recalled, 'I was forced to go and dig potatoes, which made the greatest part of a dinner to better men than myself; and if it was so with us it may easily be supposed the poor soldiers had harder times of it.' Berwick had laid waste the countryside and burnt Newry, although he made no attempt to harass Schomberg when he marched through the Moyry Pass. On September 7 Schomberg's army camped in marshy ground a mile north of Dundalk. Storms had delayed Schomberg's supply ships and the rainfall, lack of proper food and general conditions, created serious illness among the Williamites. Schomberg's cautious mind, fond of elaborate planning and unwilling to improvise and make a sudden dashing advance, had given James time to organise an army of 20,000 men to meet him. By September 20, James had marched his army almost to Dundalk and Schomberg prepared for defensive action rather than offensive. 'I do not see why we should risk anything on our side', he wrote to William. The Jacobite commanders found Schomberg's inaction incomprehensible. According to Jean-Antoine de Mesmes, Comte d'Avaux, Louis' ambassador to the Jacobite court, Schomberg would have attacked if he could have relied on the Huguenot regiments who were not too affected by sickness, according to what a French prisoner had told him. But Schomberg felt the Huguenot soldiers to be unreliable. The fact was that many of them had deserted to the Jacobites. George Story says that Schomberg's officers had urged him to attack several times but Schomberg was too cautious. William himself wrote urging an attack but Schomberg countered this with numerous complaints about supplies and the state of the roads in Ireland, pointing out that the Jacobites had twice the strength of the Williamite army. They were, he said, 'at least double the number of ours, of which a part is disciplined and pretty well armed, and hitherto better nourished'.

In fact, Schomberg's only obstacles to a swift and overwhelming victory were his own caution, the weather and disease. The Williamites, like Cromwell's soldiers before them, fell to dysentery and fever and there was an acute shortage of physicians and medicines. Many were removed to Belfast while others were evacuated to England, but conditions during the winter crossings were so bad that few arrived back alive. Some 2,000 died in the camp near Dundalk, a further 2,762 died in the hospital at Belfast and 900 died during the evacuation to England. Before spring, 1690, it was estimated that 7,000 Williamite soldiers had perished. The English public were not informed about the horrors of the campaign and the *London Gazette* continued to report on the 'excellent health' and prosperity of the army.

With winter approaching the Jacobites retired to Ardee where they too began to fall ill due to damp quarters caused by rainstorms, bad food and a lack of good medical supplies. Schomberg also retired and made Lisburn his headquarters for the winter. The Jacobites had achieved a moral victory and the army was now full of confidence. The Jacobite officer John Stevens, a captain in the Grand Prior's regiment of foot, observed that the army 'expressed a great alacrity and readiness to march towards the enemy, though most of them were very raw and undisciplined and the generality almost naked, or at least very ragged and ill shod'. Most of Ulster was under Schomberg's control, however, as most of the native Irish had fled, leaving the pro-Williamite colonists in firm control of all the towns and castles. Most of the countryside had been devastated by the war. However, Schomberg now came in for increasing criticism in England. Had he been a different type of general, a Berwick or Marlborough, he might have delivered one smashing blow to the meagre army of the Jacobites and been in Dublin before the end of September. The House of Commons were demanding a committee of inquiry and it was under these conditions that William decided he himself would have to take command of the army in Ireland.

The anonymous author of *Villare Hibernicum*, serving with the Williamite army, did not share William's censure of his commander.

Duke Schomberg was much censured by those that knew little of the matter, that he had not advanced, and fought the enemy, while his men were in heart, and they in a consternation. Or that he had not drawn off from Dundalk and retired to the north when he found bad weather coming on. But these gentlemen knew not the difficulties the Duke had to contend with. To give the enemy battle before he had been joined by Kirk's two regiments and the Enniskilleners must in all probability have been of fatal consequences as the enemy were near treble our number and were also posted to advantage; nay, this was what the enemy wanted, as appeared by this marching down to give us battle; and was it not in hope of drawing us to a battle, they never had suffered us to pass the mountains. Had he retired north before the enemy broke up, he had run a risk of having the rear of his army, at least, cut to pieces, and as to the rest, he could not have chose a more advantageous post, than the ground he encamped on. Upon the whole, it was not possible for the great general to have done more than he did. He obliged the enemy to quit all the northern parts and secured them for winter quarters for his own troops and this was all that was expected from him when he left England.

William, however, felt that Schomberg lacked the authority and vigour necessary for a decisive victory. Only he would be able to provide the organisation and impetus to overcome the 'incorrigible slowness and neglect' of Schomberg's administration. At dawn on June 4 he had set out from London with a large train and spent three nights on the road to Chester. The crossing was a bad one as the author of *Villare Hibernicum* noted. 'The wind was very brave and the weather foggy, so that the Fleet often cast anchor to stop the tides and did not reach Ramsey Bay at the north end of the Isle of Man till ten of the clock on Friday night, being the 13th.' The next day saw a change in the weather. 'On Saturday, the 14th, the wind blew pretty fresh and by half an hour after noon the same day His Majesty arrived in the Bay of Belfast, from whence he sailed into the Lough of Carrickfergus with the whole fleet that attended him, and about three went ashore at the said town.' An eye witness said that there were 700 ships in the lough which resembled a forest.

With William came his closest adviser, a man who had done more than most to point out how important it was to bring the war in Ireland to a speedy end. This was the forty-one-year-old Dutchman, Hans Willem Bentinck, later to be Earl of Portland. Hans Willem was the son of Henryk of Diepenheim in Overyssel, and had been attached to the Orange household as a gentleman of the Prince's bedchamber. For many years his advice had been invaluable to William. There were numerous other dignitaries such as James Butler, the young second Duke of Ormonde, the second but eldest living son of Thomas, Earl of Ossory. Ormonde had been one of those who had voted not to depose James and make William regent but he had bowed to the inevitable, was created Knight of the Garter by William and became commander of his English Guards' regiments. There was also Charles Montagu, the first Duke of Manchester, captain of the yeoman of William's English Guards; then Richard Lumley, the Earl of Scarborough, a Catholic turned Protestant, who was one of the prime movers in asking William to England and now commander of the First Troop of the English Horse Guards. Henry Sidney, of whom Bishop Gilbert Burnet said 'the whole design' of inviting William had been in his hands, was commander of a regiment of William's English Foot Guards. Now, aged forty-nine, Sidney was indolent but still an intriguer. Burnet felt his part in the revolution was an accident in that he had been a confidant of William. Finally, Robert Harley, the Earl of Oxford, was there with a place on William's general staff, together with Thomas Coningsby, the Joint Receiver and Paymaster-General of the army.

The list of dignitaries was impressive to the colonists. Important among William's followers was Prince Georg of Daamstadt, the thirty-seven-year-old brother of Christian V of Denmark and husband to James' daughter Anne. Georg was the second son of Frederick III of Denmark and Sophia Amelia, daughter of Georg of Brunswick-Luneburg. As a youth he had travelled in Europe and had some naval training, seeing active service. In 1674 there had been an attempt to place him on the Polish throne which had failed because of his aversion to Catholicism. On July 28, 1685, he had married Anne and settled in England.

Despite his Lutheran upbringing he had been quiet while his father-in-law began to change the constitution. James seemed to have an affection for Georg and when, after Georg had supped with him and then ridden off to join William following his landing, James had sadly remarked 'so *est il possible* he is gone too?' he ordered Georg's servants and baggage to be sent after him. Georg became a naturalised English subject in April 1689, and was made Baron Ockingham, Earl of Kendal and Duke of Cumberland by William. But William was always extremely cold towards him. Georg was 'very fat, loves news, his bottle and the queen' said Burnet when Georg's wife Anne succeeded to the throne. He was an intelligent man who was deeply interested in navigational problems. Burnet said he 'knew much more than he could well express' and 'his temper was mild and gentle' and 'he was free from all vice'.

William and his party were greeted by the Duke of Schomberg at Whitehouse, the residence of Sir William Franklin, husband of the Countess of Donegal, which stood on Macedon Point, on the lough shore halfway between Carrickfergus and Belfast. Constantijn Huygens noted in his *Journaal* that William was very cold to the old duke. Most of William's generals gathered at the Whitehouse to be received by William. Among them was Meinhard, Count Schomberg, the duke's third son who had recently been appointed General of Horse. Meinhard had visited Ireland during the previous year. He had once been a naturalised French subject but had joined the side of the Grand Alliance as a general of horse in the army of Frederick William, Elector of Berlin. Meinhard had returned to Ireland on June 6, with a formidable artillery train, to take up his new command. Also at Whitehouse was the popular German commander of the 7,000 strong Danish division, Lieutenant-General Ferdinand Wilhelm, Duke of Würtemberg-Neustadt, who had been a soldier since the age of sixteen. There were other commanders such as Godert, Baron de Ginkel of Utrecht, the Count of Solms-Braunfels, Count Henry Nassau, Sir John Lanier, Gustavus Hamilton, the commander of the Enniskillen regiments, and civil dignitaries such as George Clarke, William's Secretary at War in Ireland, Jean Payen de la Fouleresse, the ambassador from Christian V of Denmark, Sir Robert Southwell, Secretary of State for Ireland and numerous others.

Having received them, William then rode on to Belfast in

Schomberg's coach amid crowds of cheering colonists and soldiers. A second coach, organized by Schomberg, brought other dignitaries who had landed with William. At the north gate of the town the members of the Corporation of Belfast met him in their robes accompanied by the redoubtable figure of the bishop-elect of Derry, George Walker. Formerly rector of Donaghmore, Co Tyrone, he had been governor of Derry during the grim days of the siege and now, 'notwithstanding his age and profession, accompanied the colonists of Ulster to animate their zeal by exhortation and example'. A civic welcome meant a speech of some kind and William disliked speeches. At the age of thirty-nine, though he had spent many years learning the language, his English was still defective. He lacked confidence when he spoke it and refused to write it. This gave rise to descriptions of his being cold in demeanour, blunt, even repulsive in address, because an imperfectly mastered language can make even the simplest of conversations sound stilted and unfriendly. But a speech was expected and the newssheet *A Full Account of King William's Royal Voyage* reflected the briefness of his address. William is reported to have stated:

. . . that he had now made another voyage by sea and exposed his person a second time for the benefit, ease and advantage of his good people of England, Scotland and Ireland. And more particularly in order to the effectual reducing of the kingdom of Ireland to its due obedience, that his good subjects may not only be rescued from the present force and violence but be settled in a lasting peace, safety and prosperity putting his trust in Almighty God (who hath by His marvellous providence hitherto preserved and conducted them in all their great affairs), and he would vouchsafe a special blessing on his present most just and righteous undertaking and thereby consummate the deliverance of these kingdoms. In order for which he had, by his royal proclamation, commanded a fast to be kept throughout the kingdom of Ireland for imploring the blessing of Almighty God on his person and army during the present war there.

According to Samuel Mullenaux, a physician serving with the Williamite army:

At night the streets were filled with bonfireworks which were no sooner lighted but the alarm signal was given by discharge of guns so planted that from one place to another of the army's several winter quarters throughout the whole country in our hands, in a few minutes, all places had been noticed of the King's arrival, and in a very few hours, made bonfires so thick that the whole country seemed in a flame; so that the enemy could not but see the cause to their eternal grief.

The guns were heard by Colonel Sir Thomas Bellingham, son

of Captain Henry Bellingham of Kendal. Bellingham had relatives with Irish estates and had served in the country from August to November 1689, returning to Preston before going back to Ireland in the spring. He recorded in his diary:

A great shower of rain after dinner, about which time we fancied we heard some great guns off from Belfast which we hoped are for the King landing. Here came James Hunter, a Quaker, quarter master of Levison's dragoons. The King had landed at Carrickfergus.

Captain Rowland Davies, the chaplain to Lord Cavendish's regiment of horse recalled that on hearing the news he had ridden to Belfast. Joining forces with several fellow officers from the regiment they went to the quarters of their Lieutenant-Colonel, had a bonfire, saw the fireworks and 'passed the night joyfully'.

The scenes of rejoicing were witnessed by Jacobite agents who immediately set out for Dublin. They had also to report that William had brought few English troops with him and this, they reasoned, was because he did not want to widen the breach between Ireland and England. He had also brought £25,000 with several tons of tin halfpence and farthings and given express orders to his Paymaster-General Thomas Coningsby to pay all the troops by June 19. Therefore, June 19 was the day the Jacobites could expect the great army of William to begin to move southwards to engage their forces.

Early on the morning of Sunday, June 15, William dutifully attended a service of public worship in the parish church in Belfast's High Street. Here he listened to Dr. Royse's somnolent tones preaching a sermon on Hebrews II, verse 33 'who through faith subdued kingdoms, wrought righteousness, obtained promises, stopped the mouth of the lion, quenched the fires of violence . . .' with Dr. Royse airing the platitude that this applied to William himself. William must have smiled a little at the deep religious fervour of the colonists. Although he had been 'converted' to the Church of England in 1688 it had been for purely political reasons and while his upbringing, under Dr. Cornelius Trigland, had been in the strict Dutch Reform Faith, William was very flexible on religious matters, especially when it came to political expediency. He had even had the Catholic Mass sung daily at his chapel at Orange to gain political advantage.

Following the service he greeted several of his officers. In fact

all the officers of Lord Cavendish's regiment were presented
including Captain Rowland Davies who recorded that he kissed
William's hand. The officers then retired to Rourke's where, says
Davies, they dined at 4s. each.

'if no other unexpected thing prevents it'

On Monday, June 16, Lieutenant-General James Douglas
arrived in Belfast with a consignment of arms and ammunition
for the Williamite army. Douglas was a Scotsman of whom
James was to write bitterly in his *Memoirs*: 'He was the first
Scotsman that deserted over to the Prince of Orange and from
thence acquired the epithet (amongst honest men) of Proto-
rebel, and has ever since been so faithful to the revolutionary
party, and adverse to the King and all his advisers, that he laid
hold on all occasion to oppress the royal party and interest.'

That Monday was 'a hot, close day' according to Bellingham
who arrived in Belfast at 6 a.m. The Duke of Schomberg and
Major-General Percy Kirk introduced William to Bellingham
later that day and Bellingham pledged his loyalty to William
'whose hand I kissed and he promised to remember me'.
Remember Bellingham he did, for Bellingham received a commission to serve on the general staff as an aide-de-camp and,
since he was very familiar with the country, he acted as personal
guide to William on more than one occasion.

The day was spent in organising the troop dispositions and
unloading the arms and ammunition from the ships. That afternoon Captain Rowland Davies went to the mountains to
conduct a burial service for a Corporal Smith of Captain
Coote's troop of Lord Cavendish's regiment 'which I did at an
old burying place within a half mile of Belfast called Shankhill'.
On the way back to his lodgings Davies saw William, with an
escort of his Dutch Guards, returning from a review of his
artillery train, 'above forty pieces'. In fact William's artillery
consisted of upwards of some fifty pieces from field guns to siege
guns. Artillery had fallen out of use in England during recent
years. Indeed, it had not been taken seriously until the first half
of the seventeenth century and then its development was con-
fined mainly to Europe. Gustavus II Adolphus of Sweden

introduced several new types of weapons including, in 1626, a leather gun which had a bore of copper tubing but an external casing of leather. This gave it a mobility and effectiveness on a field of battle but the shooting of its nineteen-pound balls caused it to become overheated after a few shots. When William arrived in England his artillery greatly impressed the English who had not developed it since Cromwell had used it in his sieges.

William's artillery consisted of some thirty-six field guns. These were basically demi-culverin with balls of six to twelve pounds but he also had several twenty-four pounders and some nineteen pounders, together with half carronades and howitzers or mortars, mainly for siege purposes. Backing this heavier artillery were little three pounder 'drakes'. The guns were usually charged in a highly dangerous manner, directly from the powder barrel, and few could fire more than fifteen shots per hour. William was greatly appreciative of correctly handled artillery for he realised that it could have a decisive effect on a battle. Nevertheless, the artillery was in poor standing in the armies of William and James because it did not 'belong' to the army. The expense of maintaining a technical force was exorbitant and only a limited number of gunners were maintained as regular troops. To augment them a number of civilian labourers and drivers were pressed into service and because these were civilians rather than soldiers they frequently deserted when the going became too tough. As many armies began to recognise this experience they realised the importance of making gunners, matrosses, fire-workers and drivers subject to the same military discipline as the rest of the army.

At the time of the Boyne the standard manuals on artillery were still Nicolo Tartaglia's works, such as *La Nova Sciento Invento*, published in Venice in 1557, and Bourne's *Art of Shooting Great Ordnance* published in London in 1578. As for the conduct of gunners employed in the army, their standard reference work was Cyprian Lucar's *Shewing the Properties, Office and Duties of a Gunner* which he included as an appendix to his English translation of Tartaglia's works, published in London in 1588. Lucar wrote:

A gunner ought to be sober, wakeful, lusty, hardy, patient, prudent and a quick spirited man, he ought also to have good eyesight, a good judgement and perfect knowledge to select a convenient place in the day of service, to plant his Ordnance where he may do most hurt unto the enemies and be least annoyed by them.

Also, a gunner in time of service ought to forbid with meek and courteous speech all manner of persons other than his appointed assistants to come near his pieces, to the end that none of his pieces may be choked, poisoned or hurt, and he ought not for any prayers or reward lend any piece of his gunmatch to any other person because it may be hurtful to him in time of service to lack the same.

Also, if a gunner charge his piece with cartridges, he ought to set them upright in a tub or some other wooden vessel which (though it seem to stand in a place out of danger for fire) should never be uncovered for any longer time than while the same cartridges are taken out one by one to charge the piece. . .

Also, every gunner before he shoots should consider whether the air is thin and clear or close and thick, because a pellet will pass more easily through a thin and clear air.

Also, every gunner ought to know that as it is a wholesome thing for him to drink and eat a little meat before he doth discharge any piece of his ordnance because the fume of saltpeter and brimstone will otherwise be hurtful to his brains, so it is very unwholesome for him to shoot any piece of ordnance while his stomach is full. . . .

Such were the instructions to William's gunners whose artillery far outweighed James' collection of some dozen or so cannon. Williamite morale was greatly improved at the sight of the great guns, some of which had to have as many as eight pairs of horses to draw them. More than a thousand horses were needed to draw the entire artillery train and its baggage.

That same Monday morning, June 16, James left Dublin for Ardee where the main part of the Jacobite army was encamped. An anonymous 'Person of Quality' who published on July 17 a memoir of the events leading to the battle, wrote that 'King James marched out of this town to join them [his army] with about 6,000 French Foot, most old soldiers, excellently well armed and clad, one regiment of these were Dutch and Protestants, and were observed carefully, for fear of deserting'. It could well be that this was not a Dutch regiment at all but Conrad von Zurlauben's Blue Regiment, the largest of the French contingent which consisted of two battalions of mainly German and Swiss soldiers, some of whom had been taken prisoner during the previous year's campaigns against the Grand Alliance, while others had been taken from a captured ship and given the choice of fighting for Louis and his allies or rotting. Naturally, the great majority had chosen liberty in the army where they could watch for the first chance to desert. Among the other regiments that marched out with James were a Walloon regiment and three new French regiments which had landed in Cork on March 12 to replace Justin MacCarthy, Viscount Mountcashel's five regiments of some 5,387 men who had been sent to France earlier that year to form the nucleus of the famous Irish Brigade of the French army.

James left Dublin in the charge of Simon Luttrell whom the Duke of Berwick described as 'an honest man'. He was the eldest son of Thomas Luttrell and had married Catherine, daughter of Sir Thomas Newcomer in whose regiment he was made a lieutenant-colonel in 1672. Two years later his father died and he succeeded to the family estates at Luttrellstown, Co. Dublin. He had levied a regiment of dragoons for the Jacobite cause and James rewarded him by making him Lord-Lieutenant of Co. Dublin and military governor of the city. Simon's younger brother, Henry, was colonel of James' 6th regiment of horse. There was some relief at the departure of the French soldiers for they had acted in a very high-handed manner in the city, offending its Protestant citizens by displays of blatant sectarianism. This placed James in an awkward situation for his attempted wooing of the Protestants was totally destroyed by the behaviour of the French. At one point M. le Comte de Lauzun, the commander of the French division, had boxed the ears of Simon Luttrell, causing little fraternity between the Jacobite generals. As James marched out of Dublin the county militia of some 6,000 men marched in under the command of Colonel Denis MacGillicuddy.

The 'Person of Quality' noted: 'We expected the Irish would have been much cast down upon King James leaving this town, and the certain news of King William's arrival, but we found the contrary, they triumphed and rejoiced as if they had got King William in a pound and the day were their own.' Rumours had much to do with the high morale of the Dublin Jacobites and one rumour had it that 100,000 people were about to rise in England, while William was out of the way, in an attempt to re-establish the old Commonwealth republic. Some said that the French Fleet would either cut William off from England or would be landing reinforcements near Dublin. The Williamite sympathisers in the city were also confident and the 'Person of Quality' expressed their general view that if the Duke of Schomberg managed the campaign the Jacobite army would have little chance of success 'if no other unexpected thing prevented it'.

'Our grave concern in this place', wrote the 'Person of Quality', 'was how we should be preserved from being plundered and burnt, in case of the defeat of the Irish army, this we thought could only be done by the English pursuing the victory close (for by a particular providence, the Irish had neglected all this time to fortify this place!)' What was not known was that James had rejected the idea to abandon and burn Dublin as 'too cruel'. Lauzun, acting on the instructions of Louis' minister for war, the Marquis de Louvois, had urged James not to attempt a full scale battle with William but to try to 'wear down' the army, suggesting a withdrawal and the burning of Dublin before it fell to William. As Lauzun wrote on July 16 to the Marquis de Seignelay, the minister of marine, James had utterly rejected such a proposal.

By the time James reached Castletown Bellow, near Dundalk, where the main party of his army was encamped under command of the French Lieutenant-General of Horse, Lery de Girardin, he had made up his mind to fight for Dublin. His Captain-General, the Duke of Tyrconnell, wrote to Queen Mary of Modena that Monday, stating that the Jacobites would have to stand before Dublin, 'for if we be driven from it and this province lost, there will be little hope of keeping the rest long'. Tyrconnell realised the difficulties facing the Jacobite army and pointed out to Mary of Modena that 'the army we have are not so numerous as his (William's) nor so well armed, but our men are in good heart, we have a great many brave men at the head of them that will, I am persuaded, not quit their master nor their friends in the day of trial'. Tyrconnell estimated that the Jacobite army had twenty-six battalions of foot, seven of French and twenty-seven squadrons of horse and near as many dragoons. 'All these together may amount to 25,000 men effective at least.' At this stage, with reinforcements still arriving in Belfast, Tyrconnell added 'that the Irish army has no full account of the strength of the English army'.

The estimation of the 'Person of Quality' that 'the whole Irish army encamped made about 36,000 all well clad and in good heart, both horse and foot, besides 15,000 more which remained in garrison' was merely an exercise in propaganda to give more weight to the Williamite victory.

The best estimate was that the Jacobites could field some 25,000 troops for many of the regiments were not filled up to full quota, the majority being under two hundred strong and recruited hastily that spring. The dragoon regiments, for example, were little more than civilians in uniform and, indeed, the majority had no uniforms at all. The only seasoned troops were the French contingent, the regiments of Zurlauben, Biron, Bouilly, Tirlon and Chémerault, but even these were not up to full strength and Irish troops had been drafted in to fill up their numbers. A few of the regiments, such as Sarsfield's Horse, Galmoy's Horse and Lord Antrim's Foot had seen action in Ulster but the greater number had never stood under fire.

Supplies of arms and ammunition were scarce. Those muskets that did work only had four rounds apiece. The French had landed supplies in March which were deficient in quality and in quantity. Colonel O'Kelly observed that the majority of foot soldiers were armed only with an iron-tipped staff. The standard weapon among the Irish infantry was merely a scythe. A Jacobite broadsheet, printed to bolster morale among the Irish troops, explained how the gleaming scythes struck terror into the enemy. But some of the soldiers did not even have such weapons as these and had to rely on wooden sticks with sharpened points. As for the artillery, the Jacobites had a total of a dozen cannon, mostly six pounders, one eighteen pounder, one twenty-four pounder taken from Dublin and a few mortars with high trajectory shells which would be useless in a standard field battle. There was little powder or shot to keep them in action. Armaments were not the only concern. There was a lack of tents and food and most of the Jacobite soldiers had to live off the land as best they could. In short, the Jacobites were a pauper army and this did not make for high spirits, especially after the loss of Ulster.

One of the better clad and equipped regiments was that of Henry Fitzjames, Lord Grand Prior of England. He was the seventeen-year-old son of James and his mistress Arabella Churchill and brother of the Duke of Berwick. The Grand Prior's regiment was clothed in white breeches and jackets lined in red. The drummers were clad in blue and white uniforms and the grenadier company were in white with red loops in their caps and a badge depicting a flaming city with the motto 'The Fruits of Rebellion' underneath it. It was in this regiment that the young English captain, John Stevens, was serving. He was, according to the Earl of Clarendon, 'an honest, sober young fellow, and a pretty scholar. His father is a page of the back stairs to the Queen Dowager, and has been so far from her first landing; he awaited on my father in Spain. He is a Roman Catholic. They are good, quiet people.' It was thanks to Clarendon's plea 'to get a colours for him' that Stevens had served in the army in Portugal. When James was overthrown he had been an excise collector in Welshpool and in January of 1689 he had joined James in France and enlisted. He had visited Ireland before, visiting Drogheda in 1685 and Limerick in 1686 and once lived in Dublin 'in esteem and splendour'. He was a literary man and eventually, before his death in 1726 in exile, he had written and translated numerous works. Stevens had begun a journal on January 16, 1689, which he kept religiously to the day of the battle of Aughrim when it abruptly closed as he was outlining the initial deployments of the troops. Perhaps in the débâcle of the retreat his manuscript fell from his knapsack.

The Grand Prior's Regiment was ordered to move into Castletown Bellow, near Dundalk, on June 17 and the regiment was resting there when they were aroused between 2 a.m. and 3 a.m. by the general beat to quarters. They were then told to march north through Tallanstown and through Co. Louth, on the north-eastern fringes of the great central plain of Ireland, a place of countless monasteries and royal palaces. It was once a highly cultivated county, the fields on the large estates stretching across fertile and gently undulating ground. But now, as the Grand Prior's Regiment marched ten miles through a 'country very pleasant and a rich soil, but mostly lying waste since this rebellion broke out into open war', the soldiers found the enclosures had been broken down and the fields overgrown since there were no cattle herds left to eat the grass. They marched through Louth itself, 'a very poor, inconsiderable village', observed Stevens, 'without so much as the remains of any former grandeur, which in many parts of Ireland is to be seen in the considerable ruins that are about small places. From this poor hole does this county, esteemed one of the best in Ireland, take its name.'

At Castletown Bellow, about a mile from Dundalk, the Grand Prior's Regiment established its headquarters in the mansion belonging to Lord John Bellow, the Lord-Lieutenant of Co. Louth, whom James had also made a Privy Councillor. The march was exhausting and Stevens had some practical suggestions for his superiors.

The day proved excessive hot and the march long, for these are not like the ordinary miles of England. But what was most tiresome was our regiment bringing up the rear, which is often forced to run when the van walks at ease, and is often made more uneasy through the indiscretion of commanding officers, especially when they take up not good measures in march through defiles. Upon all halts the rear is marching up while the front rests, so that they have scarce a breathing before the drum beats to march again, unless general officers will be so kind to their men, where no danger is near, as to let them halt in columns as they march, and not oblige them still to draw up in a line.

The Jacobite army was now centring on Dundalk where James had confronted Schomberg the previous autumn. Tyrconnell's and Galmoy's Horse arrived on June 18 and there was now a feeling of elation running through the Jacobite army, that light-headedness which precedes a battle. Despite their poor arms and equipment many of the Jacobites were expressing their desire to come to grips with William. William, however, was not to be rushed. He had been up early on the morning of June 17 to review Lord Cavendish's Regiment of Horse in Belfast Park. Captain Davies noted that 'he rode between all ranks and then, taking a stand before the left squadron, we all filed off troop by troop, and marched man by man before him'. It was important, William had decided, for the morale of his troops to make personal acquaintance with them all, to meet the officers and to show them that he was prepared to share all their problems and hardships.

'wholly taken up with arming the camp'

On Wednesday, June 18, a new contingent of reinforcements arrived from Hoylake and disembarked at the Whitehouse. Among them was a French trooper named Gideon Bonnivert who liked to keep a journal of his adventures. Bonnivert was impressed by Belfast 'which is a large and pretty town, and all along the road you see an arm of the sea on your left, and on the right great high, rocky mountains, whose tops are often hidden by the clouds, and at the bottom a very pleasant wood, very full of simples (sic) of all sorts'.

Belfast was now teeming with Williamite soldiers and William's concern was to concentrate his forces in order to begin the march on Dublin. The 7,000 strong Danish division, which had arrived in mid March, was now stationed in Cos. Derry and Antrim. He ordered their corps commander, the Duke of Würtemberg-Neustadt, to mass his cavalry and infantry to the south of Belfast. That Wednesday Würtemberg-Neustadt moved his headquarters from Galgorm Castle, near Ballymena, to Lisburn. And two days later the Danish corps joined forces at Tanderagee to the west of Armagh.

The feeling of expectant excitement had now spread itself as far as Dublin and while the Jacobites 'were so open as to tell their Protestant friends very lately that they would be glad to go to mass within this twelve months' the military governor, Luttrell, was none too sure about the security of his position. There were a great number of pro-Williamites in the city who could very easily create problems. He decided on that Wednesday to invoke the same security measures that had been taken when Schomberg began his march towards Dublin the previous year. A proclamation was posted beginning with the words: 'Whereas several disaffected persons of the Protestant religion are of late come to this city of Dublin and some of them armed with swords, pistols and other weapons, contrary to His Majesty's commands, by His Majesty's proclamation bearing the date the 20th July, 1689 . . .' Luttrell now forbade more than five Protestants to gather on the streets of the city. The 'Person of Quality' recalled that the proclamation was enacted on the Thursday, June 19, when Luttrell and MacGillicuddy 'ordered all persons walking the street with swords or bayonets to be arrested'. By noon all suspected Williamite sympathisers had been disarmed and in the evening lists of arrested people were checked and many were sent to prison. The 'Person of Quality' said that Protestants were now synonymous with Williamites. They were rounded up with a further two hundred from Sir Thomas Southwell's party from Galway, and taken to Round Church with all the Newgate prisoners 'where they were near stifled'. Prisoners of war were removed from Kilmainham to St. John's Church. Arrests continued to be carried out over the next few days and among those arrested on June 24 was Anthony Dopping, the Anglican bishop of Meath, and William King, the Dean of St. Patrick's Cathedral. King was no stranger to prison. An active Williamite, he had been appointed with Chancellor Samuel Foley to watch over the diocese of Dublin when, in 1689, the Williamite archbishop Francis Marsh left for safer climes in London. In July 1689, in view of such defeats as Killiecrankie in Scotland, and being driven away from Derry and out of Newtownbutler, the Jacobites had decided to round up Williamites in Dublin. King noted in his diary: 'On the 25th July, 1689, I and many others were arrested and imprisoned.' He had been released late in December. Now he was suspect again and wrote: 'I was again imprisoned with so great a flock of Protestants to at least 3,000 and there I remained until the victory of King William at the River Boyne overthrew all the professed champions of the opposite party.'

For the Jacobite army at Dundalk the early hours of Thursday, June 19, provided some excitement. About 3 a.m. the camp was roused by a general beat to arms and by 5 a.m. or 6 a.m. the entire foot regiments were standing to arms. Having mustered they were marched off a half mile down the road towards Newry. Stevens said they heard the alarm that the enemy were just down the road from their positions. The cavalry mounted and advanced. 'Several parties were sent out . . . but it proved a false alarm, the horse and dragoons soon returned to camp, but the foot continued at arms in the field till nine o'clock at night.'

While the Jacobite infantry were standing to arms, that evening William had set out for Lisburn to dine with the Duke of Schomberg and discuss strategy. Passing through Lambeg William met a Huguenot, René Bulmer, who had settled in the area after the revocation of the Edict of Nantes. Bulmer asked permission to embrace the King and William, seeing Bulmer's pretty wife, granted it with a twinkle in his eye, adding, 'and thy wife also'. Two miles from Lisburn William and his party were overtaken by a shower of rain and took shelter under some trees. A Mr. Eccles from a nearby house requested that the King and his staff use his home, refreshment was provided and William, suffering from a severe headache, stayed there until the rain stopped. The enterprising Mr. Eccles immediately renamed the house from Malone Grove to Orange Grove.

William reached Lisburn where he ate a meal with Schomberg. The talk revolved around the prospective battle. Schomberg had already written to William, before he had arrived, that the most likely place for the Jacobites to make a stand was on the River Boyne near Drogheda. He had also mentioned that in order to reach Dublin the quickest possible way, it would be best to cross at Navan, further up on the river. In this he was supported by Dan Golborne who, on May 31, had written to Sir Arthur Rawdon 'that King James has drawn down all his forces towards the Boyne upon which he makes encampment and fortifies all passes: and on this river proposes to make his defence'. Although inaccurate at the time it reflected the conclusion that the Boyne was the most suitable location for James to fight a defensive action.

After the exchange of views, William, never one for inaction, inspected the troops encamped on Blaris Moor and then rode on to the encampment at Hillsborough with Prince Georg of Daamstadt, the Duke of Ormonde and Lieutenant-General Douglas. Captain Rowland Davies, who had joined his regiment at Lambeg, rode with them to Hillsborough. The Williamite physician, Samuel Mullenaux reported that a further 2,500 horse had landed near Belfast that Friday, and Saturday, June 21, was 'wholly taken up with arming the camp' at Hillsborough.

As for the Jacobite army, Friday had been a quiet day while the foot soldiers rested from the tensions of the day before. The French regiments and some others had marched to the Dundalk camp and Stevens found time to note down the names, colours and mottoes of some of them. He reckoned that, all told, there were about 28,250 men in the camp. Saturday was not such a lazy day and there were more rumours that the Williamites were advancing. That night Stevens recorded that '200 chosen men out of five regiments, 40 from each, were sent to cover the Newry road to observe the enemy's advance'.

On Sunday, June 22, William rode from Hillsborough to Newry where he reviewed the soldiers encamped there; a force of about 2,400 horse and dragoons. Of special interest to William were the colonial regiments levied from the English and Scottish settlers, mainly in Derry and Enniskillen, under the overall command of an experienced soldier Gustavus Hamilton, the governor of Enniskillen. It was the Enniskillen

regiments that had the fiercest reputation. Consisting of three
regiments of horse and dragoons, commanded by Colonel
William Wolseley, an Englishman who had arrived with Kirk,
they had joined Schomberg at Dundalk the previous September. Their appearance surprised the regular soldiers of Schomberg's army. According to Story: 'The sight of their thin little
nags and the wretched dress of their riders, half-naked with
sabre and pistols hanging from their belts, looked like a horde
of tartars. . . .' The Enniskilleners were without uniforms for
even when they were supplied with them, they preferred to
fight in their shirtsleeves. They were also not very well disposed
towards regular army discipline. They were fiercely courageous
but, Story says: 'They could not bear to be given orders, but
kept saying that they were no good if they were not allowed to
act as they pleased. This was such a contrast to Schomberg's
strict discipline that he decided to make an exception and let
them go according to their own genius.'

The Enniskilleners were rough-riding farmers who conducted
a series of hit and run raids on Jacobite positions. The cause
they fought for was the retention of their land, their farms,
wrested from the natives at sword-point since they considered
them theirs by God-given right. In many ways they resembled
the Boers of South Africa and fought with equally deep con-
victions and severity. Enniskillen itself was a small unwalled
town of some eighty houses standing on an island between
Upper and Lower Lough Erne under the shadow of a castle.
The township had been founded by settlers under James I's
plantation scheme. Its strategic value was of tremendous
importance—a centre for the colonists of North Connaught and
South Ulster, a bulwark for defending the Erne Valley and
with a link, via Ballyshannon, to the outside world. Early in
1689 the settlers in the area had declared for William and
Mary. Tyrconnell had sent Pierce Butler, Viscount Galmoy,
and a small brigade to capture it. He had no success and withdrew, leaving behind a reputation for dishonour. Under
Thomas Lloyd, a colonist from Roscommon, the Enniskilleners
developed their talents for guerilla warfare. Several attempts
were made by Marshal Conrad von Rosen, Berwick and
Sarsfield to defeat them but, like all good guerillas, they
managed to avoid an outright conflict until they were assured
of victory. William was impressed with his rough-riders.

William III
Portrait after W. Wissing

James II
Portrait by G. Kneller, 1684–5

Friedrich Herman, first duke of Schomberg, William's Captain-General at the Boyne.

Richard Talbot, earl and titular duke of Tyrconnell, James II's Captain-General at the Boyne.
French school, 1690

Prince George of
Daamstadt
Portrait by M. Dahl, 1705

Hans Willem Bentinck,
afterwards 1st earl of
Portland, who wrote the
official Williamite
account of the battle.
Studio of H. Rigaud

Godart, Baron Ginkel,
Dutch cavalry
commander at the
Boyne, who afterwards
became William's
commander-in-chief.
Mezzotint by I. Smith
after G. Kneller

James Butler, second
duke of Ormonde,
commander of
William's English Horse
Guards at the battle.
Attributed to M. Dahl, 1714

'it was resolved to give up Dundalk'

Antonin de Caumont, Comte de Lauzun, was pressing James
to retreat. He argued that, in the first place, James was too far
from Dublin and William could easily cut him off. He pointed
out how badly armed the Jacobite troops were and that supplies
were short. James' best hope lay, he reasoned, in pulling back,
burning Dublin and marching his army away to the west of the
country, avoiding any engagement with William until his army
were in a better position or until William's army was weakened
by shortage of supplies and illness. James did not set much
store by Lauzun's advice. He had seen little active service and
had only secured his post because he was the husband of
Louis XIV's cousin, the Princess de Montpensier. Lauzun had
been an early favourite of Louis XIV and then he had 'the
effrontery to seek from the King' the hand of the Princess,
whose lover he had been for some years 'and to request that the
marriage should take place with royal magnificence'. Louis XIV
had refused and, as a bribe, offered to make Lauzun a marshal
of France, duke and governor of Provence. The Princess, whom
he had already married in secret, smuggled him out of prison in
the Castle of Pigueral, and he escaped to England. He finally
mended his relationship with Louis and was eventually given
command of the 6,000 strong French division and appointed
Louis' military adviser to James II. In turn, he relied on the
military advice of his Maréchal de Camp, Marquis de la
Hoguette. James brushed aside Lauzun's advice and told him
that his idea was to strip the country before William, using a
scorched earth policy which would considerably weaken
William before he reached Dublin. Lauzun passed the information on to the minister of war, Louvois, but felt that James was
being a little unrealistic. At the same time he was becoming
resigned to an inevitable battle, in spite of his counselling and
pleading.

The Jacobite troops that had been sent out to 'observe the
enemy's advance' rode back into camp on Sunday, June 22 and
reported on the success of the first engagement of the campaign
with Williamite troops. To prove it they had some prisoners of
which one was a Captain Farlow. In the early hours of the
morning Lieutenant-Colonel Laurence Dempsey of Lord

Galmoy's Horse Regiment, with a troop of sixty horse and some infantry troops commanded by Lieutenant-Colonel Fitzgerald of Lord Bellow's Foot Regiment, had marched up the road towards Newry. At the Moyry Pass, leading to the Cooley Mountains, which legend had it was the pass where Cuchullain defended Ulster from the armies of the rest of Ireland, the Jacobites had seen a party of Williamite foot and dragoons, which they estimated to be some two to three hundred strong. According to the Jacobite Stevens, 'it had been observed that each night a guard of horse and dragoons were sent to Moyry Pass called Halfway Bridge' and the troops had been sent off for the purpose of taking some prisoners to gain intelligence about William's dispositions.

The Jacobites had lain in ambush and opened fire on the Williamites as they rode by. According to the author of the Jacobite account, *Light to the Blind*, the Williamites retreated with a loss of some thirty dead. The Jacobites took a Captain Farlow and another officer prisoner. Stevens says 'of the rebels above sixty were killed'. On the Williamite side, Bellingham noted: 'This morning we had a skirmish with the enemy about Moyry Pass, wherin we lost above 20 men but killed more of the enemy.' Davies puts the Williamite losses at sixteen men killed and some ten wounded and taken prisoner. Of the Jacobite losses Stevens says there were 'a few wounded and fewer killed, among which was Lieutenant-Colonel Dempsey, shot through the shoulder whereof he died. I was,' he adds, 'not present at this action but had an account from some who were.' Dempsey was from an old family with estates in King's and Queen's counties.

Captain Farlow, of Colonel Stewart's Regiment, did not prove a useful prisoner to the Jacobites. On being questioned he told them that William had an army of 50,000 men. *Light to the Blind* observes: 'This, I am sure, was an exaggeration to oblige the King to fly before his enemy and leave him [William] in the country of plenty, of which Orange stood in need, not having any sustenance but what he brought with him out of England, which could not by that time be much.' Farlow revealed, however, that William was going to march with his main army through the Moyry Pass towards Dundalk. Now Moyry was a good position and a small force could hold up an entire army there, as Cuchullain had done in mythology, but

James also learnt that Lieutenant-General Douglas was going to march on Dundalk on the longer route via Armagh and Castleblaney, thereby outflanking the Jacobites. Recalling the success of the skirmish at Moyry, James wrote:

This trifling success animated the troops, and increased their ardour to engage; but it made no change in the resolution the King had taken to avoid an engagement as long as possible; in consequence of which His Majesty, as soon as he learned that the Prince of Orange had made the necessary dispositions for his march, and meant to take a strait road for Dundalk, not thinking the post he was in tenable against so superior an army, moved his camp and retired on the 23rd to Ardee, where his artillery joined him.

James' eldest son by his mistress Arabella Churchill, the dashing nineteen-year-old Duke of Berwick, approved his father's plan and pointed out 'the enemy by a short march towards its right by way of Armagh could have reached the plain south of Dundalk. Therefore it was resolved to give up Dundalk to retreat and to take up a firm position on the right flank of the Boyne'.

It was commonly felt by most Williamites that James would try to defend Moyry Pass and Davies reported that two Scottish ensigns who had deserted that Sunday, June 22, told him that this was the Jacobite plan. The Sunday was 'a hot day', recalled Bellingham, who went to visit Sir Arthur Rawdon of Moyry later in the afternoon before supping with Colonel Matthews who had just taken over the command of the Royal Regiment of Dragoons, some 406 men, from Colonel Heyford. George Story's regiment was drawn up at Loughbrickland that afternoon waiting for William to review it. He arrived with Prince Georg, the Duke of Schomberg and the Duke of Ormonde. Story noted that 'the weather was then very dry and windy which made the dust in our marching troublesom'.

I was of the opinion with several others, that this might be uneasy to the King and therefore believed His Majesty would sit on horseback at a distance in some convenient place to see the men march by him, but he was no sooner come than he was in amongst the throng of them and observed every regiment very critically. This pleased the soldiers mightily and everyone was ready to give what demonstration it was possible, both of their courage and duty. The King and the Prince had their moving houses set up and never lay out of the camp during their stay in Ireland.

Story's concern was for William's health. The Nassau family

were unhealthy, given to mysterious fevers which were certainly tubercular. Often they died young or became ill in middle age. William was no exception. He was always weak and had a constant consumptive cough, his face was sullen and bloodless and scored with the deep lines which were the product of fighting ceaseless pain. An asthmatic, he could not handle a sword or warhorse until he was nearly full grown. Even as a young man he was aware of his failing health and took remarkably good care of himself, eating simply, drinking little and going to bed early. It was this strict regime that had allowed him to live.

During the afternoon William sent a messenger to Dundalk with a warning to the Jacobites that if he found any more houses and fields burnt down by them he would give orders 'not to give quarter to a man, either French or Irish, they shall meet with'. The messenger had observed great activity in the Jacobite camp and so, later that night, a force of five hundred men were sent out 'to discover the ways and observe the enemy'. They were commanded by the Dutch Major-General Adam van der Dyn, Heer van 's Gravemoor. They did not return until the following evening and reported that the Jacobites were moving out of Dundalk in the direction of Ardee.

While the news was good for morale there were a number of internal troubles among the Williamites. The Danish corps was the centre of several disturbances over the question of pay. Wichman Hansen, War Commissioner and Paymaster of the corps, had not received any money from Jens Harboe, the Danish Chief Secretary for War, which he was supposed to have sent to the corps. Nor could Hansen raise a loan from William. The Adjutant-General, Hans Georg Walter, had reported to the Duke of Würtemberg-Neustadt that the soldiers were in a near state of mutiny. Some money was found but not enough to pay the full amount due to the soldiers. On June 22 Würtemberg-Neustadt wrote to Harboe that 'some of Prince Frederick's Regiment would not accept their pay and permitted themselves to use mutinous language'. Prince Frederick's was a foot regiment commanded by Colonel Wulff Heinrich Kalneyn, a Prussian and a stickler for discipline. As Würtemberg-Neustadt reported, 'Colonel Kalneyn arrested two who were court-martialled and one was shot'. The next day five members of Colonel Montz Melchoir von Donop's cavalry regiment had to be arrested for mutiny. Würtemberg-Neustadt reporting the affair to Harboe, commented: 'There was an attempted mutiny in von Donop's regiment because they were not properly paid. I ordered a court martial and one man was shot.'

The Jacobites were not without their desertions and mutinies. Stevens recalled that on June 22 'was taken one who received pay as a sergeant in our regiment, deserting to the enemy, and hanged at the head of the battalion. Three others who, together with the former, being all Scotsmen, had served in (Lord) Dunbarton's Regiment and made their escape from Flanders and thence over to us, went away to the rebels, which caused a reasonable suspicion that they, and some of the same stamp that were among us, came over as spies rather than to serve.'

It was early on Monday morning, June 23, that the main body of Jacobites prepared to march. One of the last regiments to leave was the Grand Prior's, which started to move off about midday. According to Stevens:

Men were detached from each regiment to receive salt meat and bread at the stores at Dundalk but it being known the King designed to abandon that place, the soldiers in a disorderly manner fell to plundering the stores, which caused no small confusion, everyone there laying hold of what he could, and running a several way. We marched back about nine miles in such manner as looked more like flight than deliberate retreat, and encamped on the north side of Ardee.

William rode a few miles beyond Newry that day to look at the area himself and returned during the evening. Story recounted an incident that demonstrated William's policy of looking after his troops.

At his coming back some brought him a paper to sign about some wine and other things for His Majesty's own use; but he was dissatisfied that all things for the soldiers were not so ready as he desired, and with some heat protested that he would drink water rather than his men should want.

Later that evening Major-General Percy Kirk sent an aide-de-camp to William to report the return of Heer van 's Gravemoor's men. A trooper had been ordered to mount to the top of the castle at Castletown Bellow and 'from thence he could see a great dust towards a place called Knock Bridge, by which he understood the enemy were marching towards Ardee'. According to Story, William 'did not seem much concerned'. The Williamites were, in fact, elated. Two more deserters were brought into the Williamite camp and said that James had an

army of only 20,000 men. 'It was the discovery of our advance
parties which made them draw off, and they gave it out that
they would stay for us beyond the Boyne.'

The author of *Villare Hibernicum* joyfully reported:

> The Irish seeing some of the horse that were the advance guard appear,
> and they thinking the whole army was approaching, immediately quitted
> their pass and fled to Ardee, burning their tents for haste, but left the town
> standing, being apprehensive that the King would be as good as his word;
> some of our advance party marched so near the enemy that they plainly saw
> them set fire to their tents and the confusion they were in.

While not accurate it would seem that the rear guard regiments, not being told the purpose of the sudden retreat, had
panicked and committed various acts of indiscipline. With
James' army now falling back before him William, on Tuesday,
June 24, gave the order for his entire army to begin the march
on Dublin.

'*We shall soon be in Dublin!*'

Although the Duke of Schomberg was still nominally Captain-
General of the army, William left it in no doubt that he and he
alone commanded. William had not even consulted Schomberg
on the route he intended to take towards Dublin and the friction
between the two men was decidedly marked. The Duke's son
Meinhard, Count Schomberg, had overall command of the
cavalry while the Count of Solms-Braunfels was designated
commander of all the infantry regiments. William planned to
march in four divisions, the vanguard would be under the
command of Lieutenant-General James Douglas, the right
wing of the army would be commanded by Major-General
Percy Kirk, the left wing would be under the joint command
of the Count of Solms-Braunfels and Lord Oxford, while the
main body would be under William's personal command
assisted by the Duke of Schomberg and Heer van 's Gravemoor.
On paper the army numbered 9,300 horse and some 34,560 foot
but many regiments and troops had been detailed for garrison
duties and when the army was reviewed at Finglas, near
Dublin, a few days after the encounter on the Boyne it numbered nearly 35,000 men, including both horse and foot.

The pride of William's army, so far as he was concerned, were his Dutch troops. He had nine regiments of Dutch horse, his own Horse Guards numbering about 150 men, Bentinck's regiment of 352 men, and the regiments of Ginkel, Monopvillans, Scholks, Van Oyen, Reidessels, Bancour and Nyenbuys with an average of 175 men each. There was also a cɪɪck regiment of Dutch dragoons, some 611 men, commanded by Colonel Eppinger. The Dutch infantry were also numerous. As well as his duties as commander of all foot regiments, Solms-Braunfels had personal command of William's cherished Dutch Blue Guards. The Guards consisted of three battalions plus two companies of cadets numbering in all 2,000 men. Five other Dutch regiments, with muster strengths of between 490 to 650 men each, completed the Dutch contingent, including a regiment of Brandenburgers.

Aside from the Dutch, the next biggest national contingent were Würtemberg-Neustadt's Danish corps with three horse regiments and eight foot regiments. There were also three French foot regiments, mainly Huguenots but with their numbers filled up by French catholics, commanded by Colonels Cambron, Caillimote and La Mellonière. A few months before, William's officers had tried to weed out all the French catholics from these regiments for fear of desertion when they met up with their fellow countrymen. The French contingent also numbered two horse regiments commanded by the Duke of Schomberg and his son Meinhard.

The English and the colonial regiments made up only one third of the army, reportedly consisting of 13,315 men. William had two troops of Horse Guards at a strength of 140 men each, plus eight other horse regiments, including Colonel Wolseley's Enniskillen horse. With Colonel Matthews' Royal Regiment of Dragoons were three other English dragoon regiments, Levison's, Gwynn's and Sir Albert Cunningham's, each with an average of 260 men with the exception of the Royals with a total force of 400 men. There were also twenty-three foot regiments which included Gustavus Hamilton's Enniskilleners plus contingents from Derry, Newtownbutler and Belfast which were commanded by the Lords Meath, Lisburn and Drogheda.

Although the army was well armed and supplied there was always the danger that the French Fleet of Admiral the Comte de Tourville would cut off its supply lines to England, and therefore an early and decisive victory was needed. A 'scorched earth' policy such as James originally envisaged could spell disaster if William was forced to spend precious time marching about the country with tenuous supply lines and no way to live off the land. Therefore, with his army outnumbering the Jacobites and with its superior arms and discipline, William felt the sooner he could engage the enemy the quicker would be the victory.

The general weapon amongst William's foot soldiers was a musket with a three foot six inch long barrel which weighed eleven pounds and two ounces. From its three quarter inch bore it fired a shot that weighed just over one ounce. At a range of three hundred yards it was an ineffectual weapon so it was usual practice to withhold fire until the enemy were a few yards away. But this musket, a crude and cumbersome weapon, was fired by matchlock. This mechanism was triggered by a length of match, a cord boiled in vinegar to keep it slow burning, which had to be lighted at the prospect of action and kept alight. In rain or windy weather this could create numerous problems. To fire the weapon the foot soldier had to take a charge of powder (he was usually issued with a dozen ready prepared charges before a battle) which he rammed down the muzzle. This was followed by the shot, a heavy lead ball, that was quite likely to roll out of the barrel if the soldier aimed his musket low. A short length of lighted match was then fixed in the cock, a pinch of gunpowder was placed as a primer in the pan, into which the cock came down with a snap as the trigger was pulled. In windy weather this was a more than hazardous experience because a spark could cause the primer to explode prematurely.

The lessons of the New Model Army of the English Civil War days were still remembered by a number of William's English commanders who instilled into their foot regiments the art of volley fire, under which the musket became a formidable weapon. Some enterprising colonels had trained their men to load and fire in unison at the beat of a drum, copying the Swedish practice whereby three ranks of soldiers could fire a salvee—the first kneeling, the second stooping and the rear rank standing. More commonly, though, they taught their men to stand in ranks where, after firing, the front rank was immediately replaced by a second rank and so on, whereby each rank could reload before they returned to the front.

The far more efficient flintlock mechanism, generally used in hand guns, was more expensive and therefore more scarce among William's foot soldiers. Only the Danish foot were completely fitted out with the weapon, as flintlocks had replaced matchlocks during the Danish war with Sweden in 1675-9. In some of the foot regiments many soldiers carried a pike as well as a musket. Usually it was a weapon sixteen feet long with a heavy iron head. The pike was to be used mainly for repelling cavalry charges against which the foot were almost defenceless. When cavalry charged the pikemen gathered in the first ranks and sustained the initial shock of the charge with levelled pikes. When it came to closer fighting the foot soldier would usually try to club his enemy with his musket rather than rely on the cheap swords issued to the common foot soldiers which were liable to break easily. But very few of William's foot carried the pike. After the Civil War it was thought to be an obsolete weapon and it had been abolished among the Danish corps by a royal decree of 1689. The Danes replaced it by the introduction of the bayonet, a French weapon, which one fixed to the muzzle of the musket. It would be three years before the English foot soldier generally adopted the bayonet and so most of William's foot regiments were totally without defence from the Jacobite cavalry.

William's horse, because of its international composition, had a variety of battle tactics. The Dutch cavalry usually relied on its firing power rather than on a charge. This 'Dutch drill' consisted of trotting forward in ranks of five to ten deep with pistols levelled. Halting close to the enemy they would discharge their pistols rank by rank, with each rank trotting to the rear after firing in order to reload. The Danes, like the English horse, placed their faith in a swift charge into the midst of the enemy using the sword. Some commanders remembered the tactics used by Cromwell who used the weight of his horse to disperse the enemy rather than shooting or the use of the sword.

Compared with the Jacobites the Williamites were decidedly better clothed. There was no such thing as a standard uniform but each of William's regiments, except the colonial ones, were provided with a uniform, usually at the expense of the colonel of the regiment. The uniforms varied and were sometimes duplicated by the enemy, which, in the heat of the battle, could lead to many difficulties. For example, the Dutch Blue Guards could easily be mistaken for the Jacobite Zurlauben's Blue Regiment because of their common blue uniforms, and the white uniforms of Cambron's Huguenots could easily be mistaken for the similar white uniform of the Grand Prior's Regiment or, indeed, the French White Regiment. In battle each side would wear, in addition to their uniform, some distinctive badge of identification. Even so, as the Williamites were to find out almost to their cost, the similarity of uniforms was hazardous.

The Williamite army therefore consisted of experienced, disciplined troops, mainly veterans of the European battles, led by tough professional officers. They were well armed, well clothed and, at that moment, well supplied. They outnumbered the Jacobites by ten thousand men and had artillery support far outweighing anything the Jacobites could provide. Above all, they had a high morale.

On the morning of Tuesday, June 24, the regiments assembled at their various quarters. Before the order was given to march a proclamation signed by William was read at the head of each regiment. No officer or common soldier was to resort to looting or was to take any article whatsoever from either the colonists or natives. They were not to forcibly requisition horses that were being used by traders to provision the army. They were not to commit any outrages against the civilian population, colonist or native. Punishment for any such offences would be by death as would, of course, any military offences such as desertion, killing a brother officer or stealing.

On William's orders Lieutenant-General James Douglas' vanguard set out to Dundalk via Armagh and Castleblaney. Major-General Percy Kirk, with the division constituting the left wing, were to march to Dundalk followed by the right wing under Solms-Braunfels and Oxford. Once through the Moyry Pass they would split into their respective divisions. They would then be followed by the main body. The Captain-General of the army, the Duke of Schomberg, was more than upset when the orders were related to him by the twenty-nine-year-old George Clarke, William's Secretary at War in Ireland. Schomberg's plan of advance had been to split the army into two columns, one marching to the west through Belturbet in

Co. Cavan to Kells or Trim, and the other marching to Dundalk by the Armagh route. William had apparently dismissed the proposal without any consultation with Schomberg. George Clarke struck up a friendship with Schomberg and he recalled that the elderly duke had complained bitterly to him about William's behaviour. Clarke, who had once been described as 'a pitiful proud sneaker and an enemy to true loyalty', maintained that he was genuinely concerned at William's treatment of Schomberg. He wrote in a memoir:

I cannot omit in this place to take notice of the little regard the King showed to that very great man, the old Duke of Schomberg. All the countenance and confidences was in the Dutch general officers, Count Solms, Monsieur Scravenmoer [Heer van 's Gravemoor] etc. insomuch that the duke, who commanded next under His Majesty, was not so much advised with about the march of the army, as he complained to me himself while we were at Belfast, and said if the King had supposed that he had not been entirely negligent in informing himself of the country that winter, he would have thought it fit to have asked his opinion which was the most proper way for it to advance, and if he had he should have told His Majesty the difficulties he might probably meet with in going by Newry and that the better way was by Armagh and the Fewes etc. but that he had never till then heard so much of what was intended as I had told him for which he thanked me.

Indeed, I think that the duke resented these slights and ill usage so much that he was not willing to expose himself more than was proper in hopes of putting an end to his uneasiness in the manner he did.

As Captain Davies' regiment, Cavendish's Horse, was marching towards Dundalk they encountered a deserter from Colonel Dominic Sheldon's Horse Regiment who informed them that James had an army of 43,000 men waiting for them. This trooper also confirmed that the Williamite Captain Farlow of Colonel Stewart's regiment, who had been taken prisoner during the skirmish at Moyry Pass, had now been transferred to a prison in Dublin. The French trooper, Gideon Bonnivert, became confused as to the day his regiment began their march, saying that on Tuesday 'June 23' he went to Lisburn. Tuesday, of course, was the 24th of the month. The next day Bonnivert's regiment marched to Loughbrickland where they joined up with several other regiments. On the way to the rendezvous they passed by Hillsborough. Bonnivert noted 'we passed by Hillsborough, a great house belonging to the King, standing on the left hand of the road, and from thence we went to Dromore, hard by that place is the bishop's house'. The great house to which Bonnivert referred to was

Hillsborough Fort which had been built in 1641–2 by Sir Arthur Hill to command the pass of Kirwarlin, on the main Dublin to Belfast road, against Sir Phelim O'Neill's insurgents. It was made a Royal Garrison in December, 1660, and Hill was appointed constable, he and his descendants to hold the office in perpetuity.

Among the other regiments that Bonnivert joined at Lough-brickland was that in which George Story was serving. On Wednesday, June 25, Story noted that they marched from Loughbrickland to Newry where a deserter from Sir Henry Belasyse's Regiment was caught and executed. Sir Henry was the grandson of Lord John Belasyse who had fought at Edgehill during the Civil War for the Royalists and who had died in 1689 in favour with James II. Sir Henry, however, had thrown in his lot with the Williamites.

By the morning of June 25 the advance guard of the Williamites had entered Dundalk without opposition. They were elated by this easy advance. Würtemberg-Neustadt wrote to the Danish Chief Secretary for War, Jens Harboe, from Dundalk: 'The army is now assembled here. The enemy yield everywhere; if they go on like this we shall soon be in Dublin!'

'it being resolved to fall upon the enemy'

The Jacobite army had completed its withdrawal from Dundalk on June 24, marching southwards past the town of Louth and Tallanstown towards the ancient town of Ardee stradling the River Dee, which the Irish called by its more ancient name of Abhainn Bhaile Atha Fherdhia, naming it after the ancient hero of mythology, Ferdia. It was, according to the ancient sagas of the Irish, at this spot that Cuchullain mortally wounded his friend Ferdia in four days of bloody hand to hand combat, then carried his dying friend to the north bank of the river so that he could reach the bank to which Cuchullain had denied him access. A general headquarters was made for James and his general staff in the old Norman quadrangular castle. Reaching Ardee that Tuesday, Captain Stevens recorded that 'we continued in the same place and spent two last days in exercise, and teaching the men to fire which many of them had never been accustomed to before'. The two days training at Ardee were invaluable for the raw recruits but, as ammunition was scarce and the guns to fire it with just as difficult to obtain, few soldiers were privileged to have fire-arms training and most had to content themselves with wielding their pikes and scythes in an effort to learn how to counter cavalry attacks.

It was not until Thursday, June 26, that George Story's regiment marched 'towards Dundalk'. There was an alarm on the march because the Williamites 'heard great shooting at sea, which we at once looked upon to be the French and English fleets, but it was only our own fleet coming towards Dundalk'. Sir Cloudesley Shovell's fleet was, at present, the master of the Irish Sea and was following William's progress southward towards Dublin. Story's regiment made their camp a mile to the south-east of the camp used by Schomberg in his confrontation with James at Dundalk the previous year. While the camp was being established some soldiers from Lord Meath's colonial regiment saw several Jacobites observing them from a position not far from the roadway. The Williamites promptly gave chase on horseback as the Jacobites fled towards the shelter of the nearby wooded mountains. They overtook them and in the ensuing skirmish one was killed and another was taken prisoner. They returned with the prisoner 'who proved', reports Story, to be 'a Frenchman that had deserted from Hillsborough about three weeks before'. Recaptured deserters were usually hanged on the spot and although the fate of the Frenchman is not recorded it is a fairly obvious conjecture.

On the same day that Story's regiment marched into Dundalk, Gideon Bonnivert's regiment had been roused at 2 a.m. and marched towards Newry. Bonnivert fastidiously noted down descriptions of the surrounding countryside in his journal.

'Tis not to be imagined how strong, naturally, many passages are that way; and besides that, many strong tho' small forts, made by King James, which might have ruined part of our army, with the loss of but few of his own. That day was the first of my seeing the King riding in Ireland and he had then on an orange colour sash. We crossed at Newry, which was formerly a strong place but now burnt and destroyed, and encamped on the side of a hill, where the water was very scarce. We left Dundalk on our left hand, it stands by the sea, and we encamped in very rugged ground. The Enniskillen dragoons came there to us. They are but middle sized men, but they are nevertheless brave fellows. I have seen them like mastiff dogs run against bullets.

On Friday, June 27, Lord Cavendish's Horse, with Captain Davies, 'marched from Newry over the pass at Moyry where,' the captain observed, 'the enemy, if they had any spirit, might easily have stopped us for some time'. Cavendish's regiment arrived at Dundalk at 10 a.m., passing the Creggan River just below the castle at Castletown Bellow and, with the other regiments that were accompanying them, they encamped in two lines some three miles in length.

Sir Thomas Bellingham had arrived in Dundalk at 6 a.m. that morning with Major-General Percy Kirk and his staff and the Count of Solms-Braunfels. 'The town', observed Bellingham, 'is wholly deserted but strongly fortified'. Story did not find Dundalk 'wholly deserted'. His regiment was ordered to march through the town and encamp a mile further on and as they marched through the narrow streets 'we found several of the Irish that lay dead and unburied and some were alive but only just breathing'. The author of *Villare Hibernicum* seems to have been with the same contingent as Story and noted that 'on the 27th we encamped on the plains of Dundalk where we rested'.

The Williamite advance guard had reported that the Jacobites were now encamped at Ardee 'not five miles away'. Rowland Davies' regiment was one of several who were told to make ready for an immediate attack by the enemy. There came a report, according to the writer of an anonymous Danish journal, that '600 of the enemy intended to attack our advance guard'. The Brandenburg Regiment sent out forty men to reconnoitre and these returned a few hours later with sixteen prisoners who confirmed that the Jacobites were in their camp at Ardee. According to Bellingham: 'the King resolved to attack the enemy this night in their quarters at Ardee; but hearing some dragoons who were at the very gate and killed two of their men, yet the enemy are retired, and he put off this resolution. I waited on the King at supper and where he discoursed me most of the time and was extremely pleasant and cheerful.'

Cavendish's Horse had been told to stand to late that evening for the attack and Davies recalled that 'at nine of the clock every man was booted and had his horse in his hand, it being resolved to fall on the enemy, this night or in the morning early. But some Dutch dragoons, that were sent out to discover, fell into the rear of the enemy, whom they found on their march and took some prisoners and a little plunder, and, bringing us an account that they were decamped, and had quitted Ardee and gone beyond it, put a stop to our design, and all were ordered to unsaddle.'

The encounter with the Dutch dragoons had taken place that afternoon when a party of Colonel Eppinger's Dutch Dragoons had made contact with a body of Jacobite horse. Major-General Patrick Sarsfield had sent Henry Luttrell's Horse to act as a rearguard for the Jacobite army and to hold William's advance up as best they could. There was little that Luttrell's nine troops of fifty-three men per troop could do to stop the advance except merely to annoy the advance parties by harassing and trying to destroy communications. Henry, the younger brother of the military governor of Dublin, had spent some years in the French army. He was said to have possessed 'a sharp intellect, polished manners and skill in intrigue and war'. He disliked Tyrconnell which eventually caused him to change his allegiance and join William. As colonel of the Jacobite's sixth regiment of horse he had not, as yet, been very active in the war. As soon as Eppinger's dragoons were sent the Jacobite horse retired towards Ardee without seeking an engagement. George Story commented: 'I was told by a general officer of theirs [Eppinger's dragoons] since, that whensoever our army moved, the Irish had a small party of horse that knew the country and kept themselves undiscovered in some convenient place to give them [the enemy] an account of our motions and posture.'

That evening, however, William ordered out a short brigade of 1,500 horse and dragoons to ride to Ardee to see if the Jacobite camp had broken up. He was up early the next morning and with a small party of his Horse Guards followed in their wake to see the situation for himself. He returned on the evening of Saturday, June 28, having established that the Jacobite army had retreated towards the old town of Drogheda.

The Jacobite Captain Stevens observed that after being two days in Ardee 'this place fared no better than Dundalk, being plundered by our own men and left almost desolate. Before the rebellion it was an indifferent good town, but most of the inhabitants fled from their homes and allegiance and the rest either dead or left worth nothing. Here we understood the enemy was advancing.' Advancing they were. Within a few hours of the Jacobite rear guard leaving the deserted streets and buildings of Ardee the Williamite advance guard were entering. According to Davies, 'a detachment of horse and dragoons found the town of Ardee deserted'. Bonnivert said that fifteen men were taken from each squadron of his regiment to make up part of the brigade to go to secure Ardee. He was one of the troopers chosen and he recalled that 'just as we came within sight of the town we saw the dust rise like a cloud upon the highway beyond it. It was the enemy's rear guard scowering away with all speed. Some dragoons were detached to follow them, who brought back two or three prisoners and many heads of cattle.' This was on June 28 which, according to Bellingham, was a 'very hot' day. Bread and beer were beginning to run rather short as James left nothing in the van of the Williamites. At Ardee, reported the Danish diarist, some three hundred soldiers reported sick 'but all of them were able to march, though with difficulty'.

Some deserters from the Jacobites began to trickle into the camp. They were, it would appear, men from Zurlauben's Blue Regiment for they were 'Germans who had been taken by the French a year ago at Brussels'. The Danish diarist commented that the Germans were full of praise for the regularity with which they received their pay and uniforms from the French. 'They had', he wrote, 'never been short of anything else. They would not take service with us but only wanted passes to go to Germany'. Unlike the rest of the Jacobite army, the French contingent, which arrived in Ireland in March, was especially cared for and Zurlauben, in particular, seems to have been a very conscientious commander.

According to Captain Davies it was on the afternoon of June 28 that two people, a man and a woman, were seized in the Williamite camp, caught in the act of trying to poison the water for the troops 'and were killed by the mob'. Story, in contradiction, says this occurrence did not happen until the next day and he seems to have his suspicions as to whether or not they were guilty. He says the event occurred on Sunday morning when an Irishman and woman were getting water at a well near to King William's tent and soldiers became suspicious that they were trying to put poison in the water 'and so destroy the King and his army'. The soldiers lynched the woman 'and almost cut the man in pieces'. The Danish diarist was more specific in that 'two pounds of arsenic for poisoning the water were found on two spies who were captured on yesterday's march and were cut to pieces by the English'.

Captain Stevens had noted that the Jacobite army was now camped near Drogheda 'near a small village along cornfields, gardens and meadows, the river Boyne is near'. The Jacobites were now aware of the nearness of the Williamite army. Stevens wrote: 'This night no word was given but about midnight, in a great hurry, ammunition was delivered out, then orders to take down all tents and send away the baggage. This done the whole army drew out without beat of drum and stood at their arms the whole night expecting the approach of the enemy.'

Sunday, June 29, was 'an excessive hot' day according to Bellingham. The main body of the Williamite army were passing through Ardee and the author of *Villare Hibernicum* says the town was 'found miserably plundered by the enemy, they leaving nothing but the houses with bare walls except some such old bed ridden people, for murdering four of which in cold blood, a Scots soldier and woman was here hanged'.

The physician Mullenaux passed through Ardee that Sunday and he, too, found it 'miserably plundered by the enemy'. George Story's regiment 'encamped in a cornfield by a small ruined village. The town of Ardee is seated in a very pleasant soil and has been a fine, strong borough as one may see by the great towers still extant'.

The anonymous Danish diarist recalls that at daybreak Lieutenant-Colonel Karl Gustav von Gam was sent out with an English colonel and three hundred troopers to see if the Jacobites had encamped on the north side of the Boyne. In fact, the Jacobites, after their long night's vigil, had been given orders to cross to the south bank of the river. According to Stevens: 'About the break of day, no enemy appearing, the army began to march in two columns, the one through Drogheda, the other over the river at Oldbridge, and encamped again in two lines in very good order on the south side of the Boyne, between two and three miles from Drogheda, the river running along the whole front; the design to make good the passes of it against the enemy, who were too strong to be engaged in plain field till we were reinforced or they obliged to fight us at disadvantage.' Von Gam's detachment encountered two troops of about one hundred Jacobite horse and Gam wanted to attack them immediately, having superiority in numbers. He was somewhat disgruntled when the English colonel 'was unwilling, alleging that he had no orders to do so'. Nevertheless, von Gam succeeded in capturing two prisoners.

The Danish ambassador, Jean Payen de la Fouleresse, was in Ardee when he was 'informed the enemy had taken up their positions along the Boyne'. The question was, would James now make a stand? Many Williamite commanders thought that James would merely continue to retreat in good order to try to tire the Williamite army and in the hope that the sickness from want of victuals, which had already begun to show itself that day, would greatly increase. In Dublin the 'Person of Quality' wrote: 'We heard the Irish army retreated and the English were come towards Drogheda; we knew James' design was to avoid a battle as much as he could and to have walked the English army along the Boyne River, and so cross the country to Limerick, but this day we were told from the camp that the enemy seemed to press towards Dublin and King James was resolved to defend it and that therefore they thought he could not be able to keep off a battle above ten days.'

That Sunday afternoon William found time to pay a courtesy call on the Duke of Würtemberg-Neustadt and review his Danish troops. While this was being done the main body of his army had marched in three columns beyond Ardee and halted. Story recalled that 'we marched within sight of the sea a great part of the day and could see our ships sailing towards Drogheda, which certainly must needs be a real mortification to the Irish'. In Cavendish's regiment, however, the confidence of most soldiers, was not shared by all. Two men were hanged on the march, 'one for deserting', says Davies, 'the other for betraying some of our men to the enemy'. Story managed to get more details about the incident when 'a soldier was hanged for deserting and a boy for being a spy and murderer'. It seemed that two weeks before, a sergeant of Lord Drogheda's colonial regiment was gathering wood near his quarters at Tanderagee when a boy came to him and told him that if the sergeant would accompany him he could take him to a place close by where he would be able to get some herbs for food. The boy led him into an ambush and five or six Irishmen disarmed him, tied him up and carried him to a nearby croft. He had been taken into Dundalk the next day but, during the night, the sergeant had managed to escape, not without being wounded several times. A week later the same boy, according to reports, tried to lure some dragoons into an ambush at Legacory by telling them that if they followed him he would show them where to get fresh horses. One of Lord Drogheda's soldiers who had heard his sergeant's story and recalled seeing the boy, spotted him carrying out a similar attempt at ambush. The boy was seized and confessed that he had been paid half a crown 'brass' for everyone he could lure into an ambush by this method. He also confessed 'that he observed as he went amongst our regiments how they lay and what condition they were in, both as to health and other matters'. He further confessed to killing a dragoon by stabbing him in the back while his father held him. Story was present when the boy made his confession and observed 'he spoke English and Irish both very well' and when the time came for him to be hanged 'he was very little concerned at it'.

Another rather ironic event occurred the same day. A French soldier became ill after drinking water and thinking he was dying he took out his rosary and started praying 'which one of the Danes seeing, shot the Frenchman dead, and took away his musket without further ceremony'. Obviously the Dane, like many others, did not understand the real causes of the forthcoming battle.

William now seemed very elated and, according to Story, 'he observed the country as he rode along and said it was worth fighting for'. That Sunday evening he decided to take personal charge of ordering exactly how he wanted his army encamped. Story took a little time to view the surrounding countryside.

There were none of the Irish to be seen but a few poor starved creatures who had scraped up some of the husks of oats nigh a mill, to eat instead of better food. It's a wonder to see how some of these creatures live; I myself have seen them scratching like hens amongst the cindars for victuals; which put me in mind of a story that I have read in the Annals of Ireland. Where it is said that in the year 1317 the Ulster Irish roved up and down the kingdom in a body, whilst the Scots army was down towards Limerick, and those people were so hunger-starved at last, that in churchyards they took the bodies out of their graves and in their skulls boiled the flesh and fed thereupon and women did eat their own children for hunger, so that out of ten thousand there remained at last only three hundred the reason of this plague the superstition of the time attributed to the eating of flesh in Lent, for which the curse came upon them.

Story was fond of recounting 'horror' tales about the Irish and historically little credence could be placed upon them.

That Sunday afternoon Captain Davies had delivered a homily to his fellow soldiers on Psalm cxviii verse 15 which he felt appropriate to the situation.

> Let God arise, let His enemies be scattered:
> Let them also that hate Him flee before Him
> As smoke is driven away, so drive them away . . .

Not all his fellow officers in Cavendish's Horse felt so committed, for that evening Davies learnt that a comrade Captain Haws Cross had been arrested 'and committed at the standard for suspicion of being a spy and inclined to desert us'. Davies went to his regiment's headquarters and found Captain Cross guarded by two troopers who would not permit him to speak to him, 'wherefore I returned pensive but unable to do him service'.

'It need not have come nearer!'

William's army was roused from its tents at 2 a.m. on Monday, June 30, and, according to George Story, moved off 'very early' in three columns towards the River Boyne 'which was but eight short miles off'. An advance guard of Sir John Lanier's regiment of horse was despatched to feel out the enemy's defences. The Danish ambassador was to record: 'At daybreak, on the 30th, we again broke up our camp. His Majesty caused the army to march in two columns, and placed himself at the head of the cavalry on the left wing. As we descended the small hills with which the northern part of the kingdom is studded, we discovered a very fine fertile plain watered by the Boyne.' The official reports suggest that the Danish ambassador had made a mistake when he mentioned the army marched in two columns and that the Williamites maintained the marching order of three columns.

Sir John Lanier's horse had been leading the advance since the order to march on Dublin had been given. Lanier was a veteran who had lost an eye while serving under the Duke of Monmouth in France and later had been knighted for his services, becoming governor of Jersey and lieutenant-colonel of the Queen's Regiment of Horse. Switching his allegiance to William he had, as a lieutenant-general, taken the surrender of Edinburgh Castle on June 12, 1689. He had a reputation for harshness and was responsible for the burning of a large part of the west side of Dundalk in February but proved his military capabilities by the capture of Bellow Castle where he acquired 1,500 cows and horses for the Williamite forces. There was a strong rumour that many of his soldiers were really Jacobite in sympathy and perhaps it was this that made William choose to place them in the van rather than in the rear.

William and his general staff, sensing the enemy to be near, rode after Lanier's regiment and caught up with them when they were within two miles of Drogheda. Together with the Duke of Schomberg, Prince Georg of Daamstadt, the Count of Solms-Braunfels, Heer van 's Gravemoor and Henry Sidney, William mounted the hill of Tullyeskar, a little hill to the north-west of Drogheda. From this vantage point the Williamite generals could see not only the town of Drogheda but the Jacobite encampment stretching away for two miles, in two lines to the west of the town and to the south of the river. Sir Thomas Bellingham noted laconically, 'I was some time with the King on the hill of Tullyeskar'. It was Bellingham who pointed out the principal sites to William, who surveyed the scene through a field glass.

The Williamite generals were elated. So James, in spite of the rumours that he 'was to avoid a battle as much as he could, and to have walked the English army along the Boyne river, and so across the country to Limerick', had decided to stand and fight. He had overcome not only the objections of the Comte de Lauzun and his French generals but the objections of his own Captain-General, Tyrconnell. Tyrconnell, a mere week before, had been in favour of standing and fighting William for Dublin, 'for if we be driven from it and this province lost, there will be little hope of keeping the rest long'. Now he had changed his opinion and was supporting Lauzun. 'I think Dublin's loss to us', he had written to Mary of Modena from Ardee a few days before, 'is not of the consequence as he [James] apprehends it.' Tyrconnell now supported the idea that the army should march across country to the west. 'I am not for declining the battle', he added, 'but if I do not, I confess I am not for venturing the loss of all to preserve a place which you must lose as soon as the battle is lost, and which, I think, is not of that consequence to us as is said.'

James ignored Lauzun and Tyrconnell and in this he was backed by his younger generals such as Berwick and Sarsfield. He had chosen his ground fairly well, for many of the Irish soldiers felt a special significance in standing at the Boyne since it was a sacred river. It had taken its name from Bóinn or Boand, a young girl who had, in Irish mythology, wedded Nuada of the Silver Hand, an Irish god who was the king of the mystical Tuatha de Danaan. He had led them against the tribe of the Firbolg at the first battle of Moytura at Cong, Loch Corrib in Co. Mayo, where he had lost his hand. The physician, Diancecht, had replaced it with a silver one so that he became known as Nuada Airgetlámh, Nuada of the Silver Hand. Nuada's young wife Boand was told that there was a secret well which no one was permitted to look into but, in the pride of her heart, she peered into the depths of the secret well and the water rose and overflowed, following her as she ran, fleeing until she reached the sea near Drogheda and was drowned. The path of the water formed a river which was named after her—An Bhóinn, the Boyne.

The Boyne ran eastward into the sea thirty miles north of Dublin. At the first bridge to cross it stood the maritime town of Droichead Atha, the Bridge of the Ford, which the colonists anglicised to Drogheda. The only other bridge across the Boyne was at Slane, nine miles along the river to the west. Initially the Boyne was a tidal river and shipping could approach Drogheda at high water but their draughts would have had to have been moderate. The river remained tidal until just past the hamlet of Oldbridge, a collection of some half a dozen stone houses clustered round an old, squat church some three miles upriver from Drogheda. The river ceased to be tidal where the Mattock river flowed into the Boyne from the east, just opposite Oldbridge, creating the first rapids. Just before Oldbridge, as you pass from Drogheda, the river widens to skirt round two islands, Yellow Island, an area of sixteen acres, and the lesser five acre Grove Island. At this juncture the river is flowing towards the north-east and then, by Oldbridge, it makes a sharp curve to the south-east, past the mouth of the Mattock on the east bank and Oldbridge on the west. Towards Slane the river curves round a great plain on which were ancient tumuli,

Knowth, Newgrange and Dowth, the traditional burying places of the kings of the Tuatha de Danaan. Along the river were many fords, fords that could be crossed at low tide. To the south of Oldbridge rose the Hill of Donore, which commanded the view from north to east but not to the west. The village of Donore stood a little to the south but there was one building in ruins on the hilltop, an old church, once the burying place of the Synnot family. Had James been in the ruined church at Donore during the battle, as was afterwards rumoured, he would have had little comfort in the one remaining table-top grave which bore the inscription:

> All ye mortals, who on this earth draw breath
> In health, prepare for the certain hour of death.

The Hill of Donore was steep on its western slope but it sank in gradual undulations towards the Boyne and Oldbridge.

The Jacobite army had finished crossing the Boyne on the Saturday evening, leaving only cavalry troops on the northern bank to act as skirmishers and warning parties. They had crossed in two columns, one through Drogheda and the other over the ford opposite Oldbridge. James had ordered Lord Iveagh, with his foot regiment and some other reinforcements numbering 1,300 men, to hold Drogheda. His main encampment was placed on some elevated ground to the east of Oldbridge, some distance from the river beyond the reach of artillery. The Jacobites camped in two lines from Rathmullen to Oldbridge. To protect them he had only eighteen six pounder field guns which he placed in three batteries—one battery near the road, on its western side just south of Oldbridge and almost opposite the Mattock, and two batteries opposite Yellow Island. James reasoned that the fords opposite Oldbridge would be the most likely place for William to try a crossing. The siting of the Jacobite army was a good one because James' positions on the south bank completely commanded the north bank from which William would have to launch his attack. On the north bank there were several narrow defiles which ran down to the water's edge and behind these the rising ground of Tullyallen and Townley Hall.

William's trained military eye took in the situation as he peered at the rows and rows of grey tents and the jaunty colours of the Jacobite regiments, fluttering in the slight summer breeze. Heer van 's Gravemoor laughingly pointed to the Jacobites and called them 'une petite armée' but William shook his head. The Jacobites, he answered, might have a great many men in Drogheda itself and to the south-west was a hill, Donore, beyond which many more men might be encamped. It was quite possible that the Jacobites were not showing all their numbers. However, he added, he was resolved very soon to find out what their numbers were.

Small troops of horse were sent towards Drogheda and to Oldbridge to test the strength and readiness of the enemy. According to the Danish ambassador, 'with the help of glasses it was discovered that the enemy had not suspected us to be so near for the horses of the cavalry had been turned out to graze. The "boutte-selle" was at once sounded, and we noticed some confusion in the camp.' Certainly two Williamite troopers surprised a party of Jacobites crossing the ford into Oldbridge and they managed to capture a horse and a barrel of ale. Some dragoons entered a house near the river and found some two hundred scythes stretched across the beams. An officer brought one to William to show him what sort of weapons the Jacobites were armed with and, according to Story, William 'smiled and said it was a desperate weapon'.

William's scouting party had reported that Drogheda was firmly in enemy hands and that any crossing by the bridge would have to be made by force of arms and probably with considerable loss of life. William then despatched Captain Pownel of Colonel Levison's regiment of dragoons towards Slane, where the only other bridge stood. Pownel was to ascertain if this bridge was guarded and if a ford might be made there.

The Jacobites had watched with interest as the vanguard of William's army appeared. According to Stevens: 'Early in the morning the enemy appeared on the tops of the hills beyond the river, some of the poor country people flying before them. They marched down and spread themselves along the side of the hills where they encamped, but so as we could not discover them all, a great part being covered by the higher ground.'

William had several of his regiments marched down to the river banks opposite Oldbridge. Among the soldiers was Gideon Bonnivert. 'There we saw the enemy', he wrote later, 'and were

so near them that we could hear one another speak.' It was an
odd move on William's part to march his troops into so vulnerable a position and the Jacobites did not let the opportunity go
by. A Jacobite battery of six pounders opened up on the luckless
troopers who stood their ground under the bombardment not
having received any order to retire. *Villare Hibernicum* stated
that the Jacobites fired about two hundred shots and killed
four or five men and some ten horses. The main casualties seem
to have been Dutch and the only officer was a Major Williams
of the 3rd troops of the Guards who was wounded in the arm.
Bonnivert was incensed that no order to retire was given and
'indeed, 'twas madness to expose too many good men to
slaughter without needs, for we had not artillery yet come to
answer their's'. The author of *Villare Hibernicum* maintained that
the 'madness' had a method in it for William wanted his un-
tried troops to stand under fire to see how they reacted. The
Williamites stood 'the shot of the enemy for several hours, while
they passed the shot beforementioned'. After a while William
was reported to have commented: 'Now I see my men will
stand!' Bonnivert recalled, 'we did retire confusedly behind the
hill at the sight of the enemy when it might have been better
managed'. It certainly seemed a strange and costly exercise in
judging the morale of the troops and as, according to both
Davies and Bonnivert, the casualties occurred in William's
Dutch Guards, the veterans of several campaigns, one would
have thought that William knew well how they would stand
under fire. One wonders whether the reason given by the author
of *Villare Hibernicum* was correct or whether it was merely an
excuse to cover up an error on the part of William or a junior
officer.

According to the Jacobite Stevens, the Williamites brought
their own artillery into action 'after noon' when 'they began to
play upon us with cannon and some mortars but no considerable damage was received on either side'. *Villare Hibernicum*
maintains that the Williamite artillery did not open up until
5 p.m. but Story, Bellingham and Würtemberg-Neustadt
observe that the Williamite cannonade began around 3 p.m. By
that time the entire Williamite army had marched up and
encamped around the hills of Tullyallen. A makeshift headquarters was set up in the ruins of Mellifont Abbey. And now,
while the army deployed, William instructed a battery of guns

to be set up opposite Yellow Island, just south of the road that led from Drogheda to Slane, past Townley Hall. The battery consisted of four six pounders and four howitzers, short squat guns used for shelling enemy positions at a steep angle. He also established a larger battery to the north of the road further to the east, on a hill beside a narrow defile which led past Tully-allen towards Oldbridge, which was afterwards named locally as King William's Glen.

It was the battery opposite Yellow Island that began the bombardment. The guns were dragged into place by teams of four horses, each barrel—some four to six feet in length—poking defiantly towards the river. The gunners made their assistants anchor each gun by placing rocks before the wheels to stop any forward movement, then with the tampion removed from the mouth of each cannon, a pound and a half of powder was ladled in and rammed home. Next came the six pound iron shot, then a touch of powder at the touch-hole, and the gunners stood ready. The fireworkers or gun captains sighted each gun, some by use of a quadrant or carpenter's square, and having checked on the siting stood aside and gave the order to fire. The guns roared, recoiling back on their wheels, and no sooner were they still than the crew were once more at work, sponging, ramming home the powder, the shot, and siting once more. One of the first shots, according to George Story, smashed into a house in Oldbridge and killed a Jacobite officer who lay sick there. The author of *Villare Hibernicum* says that the Williamite artillery 'dismounted some of the enemy's guns on their batteries, and with our bombs, beat down several tents next adjoining to those of the late King James and Caumont de Lauzun'. Williamite propaganda afterwards had it that James had made his head-quarters in the ruined church at Donore and, indeed, had remained there out of harm's way until he saw the fording of the river at Oldbridge. This was, of course, quite untrue. James' initial headquarters were just across the river to the east of Oldbridge. Story confirms *Villare Hibernicum*'s account by saying that a shot from the guns 'as we heard afterwards, fell nigh a crowd of great officers that were at the late King's tent and killed a horseman that stood sentinel'. Bellingham observed that the guns fired all afternoon and destroyed two Jacobite guns.

Soon after three o'clock William decided, much to the horror of his general staff, to ride down to Oldbridge and observe the situation for himself. Despite their fears for his, and perhaps their own, safety they rode with William opposite Grove Island where a small party of Jacobite Horse was stationed. William and his party halted almost within musket shot of Oldbridge. They could now observe the stone houses of the village. William saw that many were loopholed, where the enemy had made slits in the walls for their muskets, and filled with troops and that stretching along the banks of the river were several entrench- ments, some of which were still unfinished. He then moved a little way along the bank to a spot where a stream passes through King William's Glen, emptying into the Boyne, and suggested, with calm disdain for the nearness of the enemy, that the party sit down for a picnic. They had been in the saddle since early morning and so were glad of a rest. Refreshments were soon brought up.

Seeing the group of obviously high-ranking officers sitting on the opposite bank, a troop of forty Jacobite cavalry advanced down the hill and halted in a ploughed field exactly opposite the picnic party, calmly inspecting them through field glasses. According to Story, among the horsemen were five 'gentlemen of the Irish army' whom he named as Tyrconnell, Lauzun, Berwick, Sarsfield and John Parker. The Jacobites were said to have sat and watched the picnickers for half an hour and it was during this picnic that a deserter from James' army was brought to William but the man could not give them much information except that the Jacobite army numbered 20,000 men. What happened then is best described by Story:

Whilst His Majesty sat on the grass (about half an hour) there came some of the Irish with long guns and shot at our dragoons, who went down to the river to drink, and some of ours went down to return the favour; then a party of about fifty horse advanced very slowly and stood upon a ploughed field over against us for near half an hour. This small party brought two field pieces amongst them, dropping them by a hedge, in the ploughed land, undiscovered, they did not offer to fire them till His Majesty was mounted, and then, he and the rest riding softly the same way back, their gunner fired a piece which killed us two horses and a man, about a hundred yards above where the King was, but immediately came a second which had almost been a fatal one, for it grazed upon the bank of the river, and in the rising slanted upon the King's right shoulder, took out a piece of coat, and tore the skin and flesh and afterwards broke the head of a gentleman's pistol.

The two shots had been fired from a six pounder. Among the first casualties was Prince Georg of Daamstadt's horse, which was killed by a shot in the neck. The second shot, although slowed considerably by its impact with the bank, would have done a great deal of harm had it not also been blunted by William's thick leather jacket. The phlegmatic William remarked '*T'houbt niet naeder*' (it need not have come nearer). Thomas Coningsby immediately applied his handkerchief to the wound, so Lieutenant-General Douglas recalled, writing to his brother, the Duke of Queensberry, a week later. According to Bentinck's official account of the campaign, William's wound was a contusion about as big as the palm of one's hand. He lost 'near half a spoonful of blood'. According to the Danish Ambassador, Jean Payen de la Fouleresse, who was also among the party:

> Those about His Majesty thought he was dangerously wounded, but he said, with great coolness, 'it is nothing, but the ball came very near' (*ce boulet est venu bien près; ce n'est rien*). The King then asked for his cloak in order to hide the hole burnt in his coat and went on further.

William went back to his carriage to have the wound dressed. He laughed at one doctor, M. Sangredo, who wanted to bleed him and called for his own personal surgeon who applied a plaster on the wound. Having had it dressed he remounted his horse and dismissed his staff saying that he would ride round the camp with the Duke of Schomberg only and thereby make himself a less conspicuous target. Story marvelled at William's escape.

> I cannot but take notice of a singular piece of providence in the preservation of the King's person, for whatever ill effect it might have had for the future, it would have been of fatal consequence to the army at that time, if he had fallen, since, instead of our going to them, the Irish would have been ready to come to us next morning, and how we would have received them there's none can tell. I have met with several that will not believe that the King was touched with a cannon bullet at all, and if so, that it was impossible it should not kill him, but I was present when the thing happened, and therefore can affirm the truth of it, I have seen a great many odd accidents in wounds with cannon bullets and yet parties live, particularly one of my Lord Drogheda's men who had all the flesh of his right cheek shot from the bone without breaking the jaw, and he's yet alive and very well.

For a while, however, a rumour did fly around the Williamite camp that William was dead or that he was dangerously wounded. However, when he was seen riding with the old Duke of Schomberg cries of 'God Save the King!' echoed through the encampment. 'At the same instant,' recalled the Danish ambassador, 'similar shouts were heard in the hostile camp. We have since been informed that they were occasioned by a speech which King James had delivered to his troops. He exhorted them to fight bravely and assured them that he would himself fight at their head. Seeing both sides thus determined to show their mettle, we expected a bloody engagement.' According to another account, the cheer that went up in the Jacobite camp was because they thought the shot had killed William and, indeed, a report of his death was circulated in Dublin early the next morning and later reached Paris where William and Mary were burnt in effigy. The anonymous author of *The Present State of Europe* pointed out that Louis XIV's most active rival would have been eliminated had the news been true and William's close shave was the cause of several stories which were to circulate after the battle. One such story was told about the Duke of Berwick who was reputed to have seen a group of officers with William in their midst. Berwick is supposed to have turned to his fellow officers and, pointing at the Williamites, said: 'Behold a splendid opportunity for putting an end to this war! We must attack that troop and destroy the Prince of Orange!' One of his men asked who would dare make such a foolhardy attack. 'I myself', Berwick is said to have replied and immediately, followed by his officers, drawn on by his example, he attacked and defeated the Williamites but William was not among them. The trouble with this story of Berwick's heroism was that the Boyne lay between the Jacobites and the Williamites and certainly no such attack was made across the river that day. Another story, more plausible, was told to a John O'Keefe many years later by a man called John O'Brien of Sligo who had been a gunner at the Boyne. O'Keefe later published it in a work called *Recollections*. Speaking of O'Brien, he says:

He was a fine old man, and told me many interesting and circumstantial anecdotes relative to that day. One, that a gunner told King James that at that very precise moment his gun was so pointed he could at a twinkle end the dispute for the three crowns, but James forbade him and his nephew and son-in-law were thus saved.

For the rest of the day the artillery duel continued and the only other incident that Story noted was the desertion of a Frenchman.

A Frenchman of ours, that afternoon, ran thro' the river before our faces to the enemy. When they saw him coming a great many of them came down to receive him, and crowding about him to hear news, our cannon threw a bullet amongst the very thick of them and killed several, and as 'twas said the fellow himself, however, the rest made what haste they could back again.

By dusk the guns were silent.

'A tolerable good post'

Between eight and nine o'clock that evening William called a council of war of his general staff officers at his headquarters in Mellifont Abbey, the twelfth-century former Cistercian abbey two miles north of Oldbridge. The abbey had been founded by Donnchad Mac Carrol, prince of Oriel, for a band of Cistercians sent to Ireland by St. Bernard of Clairvaux. Its first abbot, Christian Ó Conairce, had been one of the first to welcome the Anglo-Norman invaders. Of late the abbey had been turned into a baronial residence but now it was deserted and falling into ruin. The main Williamite encampment spread itself around the great grey walls of the abbey buildings.

The majority of William's generals were cautious, although some of them had urged William to launch several regiments against the Jacobite positions that afternoon in a surprise attack. William, however, had dismissed the idea, pointing out, perhaps with a certain amount of humour, that he had a personal phobia about undertaking anything on a Monday. Most of William's generals had spent the afternoon, as William had done, riding along the river to seek out weak spots. The conclusion they had come to was that the Jacobite army had chosen their ground fairly well. Indeed, according to Bentinck, William had at first felt that crossing the river by the fords held by the enemy was not only a difficult task but an impossible one. A deep river lay in front of the Williamite army and beyond it was a morass. Behind the morass was rising ground, high and steep, and William could not observe exactly how many Jacobite regiments lay hidden in the dips of the ground. Hastily constructed breastworks had been erected along parts of the river and these, with the fences and small stone walls which bordered the fields, afforded more than adequate shelter for the Jacobites.

If William's soldiers succeeded in fording the river, the successive rises in the ground gave the Jacobites ample opportunity for making fresh stands and thus contesting, foot by foot, the Williamite advance. William had himself observed that the stone houses in Oldbridge had been entrenched and loop-holed. Well-placed infantry and dragoons could make it a hard contest for any troops crossing the river. The Jacobite side of the river completely commanded the northern banks, especially near Oldbridge. The main advantage for William was the fact that the river itself did not present an insurmount-able obstacle. It was easily fordable in spite of the fact that between Drogheda and Slane there were no bridges and that the river up to the Mattock, just east of Oldbridge, was a tidal river. The time of high water at full moon was about 10.30 a.m. but at the quarter moon, low water was about that hour. So the river was fordable at low tide and most easily during spring and at the neaps, the tide of the quarter moons when the water rises less and falls less. On July 1, 1690, the moon was five and a half days old, so the tides were far from extreme and the neaps were already beginning so that low tide would be around 9.30 a.m. to 10 a.m.

The main problem, therefore, lay in the fire power of the Jacobites and in the determination of their troops to dispute the crossing. Clearly William must bring the main bulk of his army against a point on the river where the Jacobites were least expecting it and in such a way that they would have no time to reinforce the area before his troops were across and the bridge-head consolidated. The Duke of Schomberg advised William that he had two options open to him. He could make a feint attack on Oldbridge while, at the same time, he could either march the larger part of his army to Drogheda, attacking and crossing the river there, or he could march to Slane, repair the bridge, which Captain Pownel had reported to have been broken up by the Jacobites, and cross it as well as crossing by a ford at Rosnaree. Schomberg favoured the latter course because Lord Iveagh and his Jacobites in Drogheda would cause William severe casualties and probably slow down the Williamite crossing for a sufficient period to enable the Jacobite army to counter attack.

Schomberg's plan to launch part of the army at Oldbridge as a feint and send the main bulk to cross at Slane in a flanking attack was supported by William's Paymaster-General, Thomas

Coningsby, as well as by the commander of his English Foot Guards, Henry Sidney. In fact, most of the English officers, such as the Earl of Scarborough, who was not only the colonel of the first troop of English Horse Guards but a Privy Councillor as well, the Duke of Manchester, the Earl of Oxford and the veteran Major-General Percy Kirk, supported Schomberg's plan.

William was not convinced, perhaps because of his estranged relationship with Schomberg whom he still blamed for the failure of the previous year's campaign. It was the fifty-four-year-old Heinrich, Count of Solms-Braunfels, whose military and nationalistic arrogance had made him detested by the English officers, who put forward the suggestion that the entire army should cross 'in the teeth of the enemy' at Oldbridge. He turned scathingly to Schomberg and said the army should not have to resort to trickery when the men were strong and brave enough to cross the river and smash all who opposed them. Solms-Braunfels' manners, his arrogance, which also went with a bravery which bordered on stupidity, caused the ire to rise among the supporters of Schomberg who stressed their support for the duke's plan even more. William, however, announced he favoured Solms-Braunfels' plan as 'bold and daring', and it was more in keeping with his own philosophy. But, being above all an astute politician, he decided on a compromise of the two plans.

The feint would be made from Slane while the main attack would be made at Oldbridge. A division, which would be commanded by the Duke of Schomberg's son Meinhard, would march towards Slane and cross the river at the ford there. Some confusion arose around this order because Lieutenant-General James Douglas, writing a week later to the Duke of Queens-berry, said the original intention was for Schomberg to cross the river at Slane, repairing the bridge, and not at the nearby ford of Rosnaree. However, Captain Pownel, of Levison's dragoons, had already reported the bridge was destroyed and Schomberg had pointed out that it would take time to repair. Also, Gustavus Hamilton had recommended four or five of his Enniskillen officers to act as guides to Count Schomberg's division to show them where the ford at Rosnaree was. So it would seem that Count Schomberg did not mistake the point at which he was to cross but the confusion probably arose later

Jacobites defending the crossings into Oldbridge across the Boyne. From a modern print by Cecil C.P. Lawson, *c.* 1930

The River Boyne at the point of William's main crossing at Oldbridge. The hill of Donore is to the left of the picture and the site of the Jacobite artillery is just behind the house on the left.

Williamite troops gaining a foothold in Oldbridge.
An etching by R. de Hodge, published by Allard Carolus, 1690

Williamite artillery firing towards the Boyne with Oldbridge to the right.
From an engraving by Theodor Maas

because Douglas was sent to reinforce Count Schomberg later on the morning of July 1 and took his reinforcing division to Slane, crossing by the broken bridge. With Count Schomberg's division, consisting of 4,000 horse, 3,000 foot and two dragoon regiments, crossing at Rosnaree about eight o'clock, William hoped that the Jacobites would think that this was his main thrust and therefore reinforce their left flank, facing Count Schomberg with troops from Oldbridge. Then, at the ebb of the tide, around ten o'clock, William would make his main assault on the village. Würtemberg-Neustadt, writing to Christian V of Denmark in the early hours of July 1 'before Drogheda', commented: 'Although the enemy is in such an advantageous position the King intends to attack about ten o'clock at the ebb tide when the water is not so deep.'

It was the understanding of the Danish Ambassador, M. de la Fouleresse, that William's intention was to surround the Jacobite army in a pincer movement, with Count Schomberg swinging round behind the Jacobites, placing himself between them and Duleek to the south, while the main Williamite thrust pushed the Jacobites back onto the Count's forces. He pointed out later that he did not think the Count had actual orders to cut off James' retreat. However, although it appears that a pincer movement was the point of the manoeuvre it also seems generally felt that William did not want to burden himself with taking James a prisoner, partly because he wished to spare the feelings of his wife Mary and partly because of the political dangers involved. He told his confidant Burnet 'that going against King James in person was hard upon him, since it would be a vast trouble both to himself and to the Queen if he should be either killed or taken prisoner'. Some felt it was this consideration that made him unwilling to take Schomberg's advice and perhaps gain a victory as complete as Ulm or Sedan, although his personal dislike of Schomberg was probably nearer the real reason.

The Williamite rearguard was to be under the command of Count Henry Nassau, Lord Auverquerque, and Hans Willem Bentinck, two men in whom William had the utmost trust. The council of war broke up with the generals agreeing that green sprigs should be worn the following day as a badge of identification for all the Williamite soldiers. Green sprigs were the usual distinguishing badge worn by both the Dutch and the Spanish in the wars in the Netherlands and therefore it was natural for William to continue the practice in Ireland. The watchword of the night was to be 'Westminster'. When the written orders, confirming the council of war's decisions, were sent round to the commanders later that night, the Duke of Schomberg remarked to George Clarke 'that it was the first order of the kind that was ever sent to him'. The split between William and his eighty-four-year-old Captain-General was widening irreparably.

After the council broke up William, tireless as ever before a battle, mounted his horse again and rode by torchlight around the encampment, stopping here and there to exchange a cheerful word with an officer or group of soldiers. William knew just how to encourage his men so that they would cheer him, throw their hats in the air and assure him they would follow him to hell and back again. Indeed, at the battle of Mons, twelve years before, William had led his men into hell. When on August 10, 1678, France had agreed terms with Holland, William had believed himself betrayed by the Dutch merchants and four days later he had attacked a French army, which was taken by surprise believing itself to be at peace with William. The French rallied behind the Marshal Duc de Luxembourg and at the end of the day William was repulsed with the loss of several thousand lives. In fact, William had never been entirely victorious in any battle, nor had he ever shown a talent as a general in the field, but he made a good officer because of his ability to instil confidence into his men and by simple acts, such as riding round the camp at midnight to ensure his men were well, he could win their undying devotion. They would overlook the Dutchman's cold demeanour, which reflected his habits of thought, silence, caution and reserve, his stilted and poor English which sometimes made a compliment seem unfriendly. They felt sorry for his feeble constitution, his constant consumptive cough, his frequent attacks of asthma, and his sullen, bloodless face scored with deep lines. Even the Duke of Berwick wrote: 'I cannot deny him the character of a great man, and even of a great King had he not been a usurper.'

James, holding his own council on top of elevated ground to the west of Oldbridge, beyond the rear of Williamite cannon shot, had no such characteristics. Like his son-in-law he had little talent as a general and had demonstrated personal bravery several times in battle, but unlike his son-in-law he lacked a certain personality which caused blind obedience in his followers. More important, unlike his son-in-law he lacked the large number of experienced generals to aid him in his planning. Perhaps it was that streak of Stuart stubbornness in the fifty-six-year-old King that made him determined to defend his position at the Boyne in spite of the counsels of Comte de Lauzun and Lord Tyrconnell. Lauzun, however, was merely acting on orders from the Marquis de Louvois, the French minister of war, who wanted William to be tied up in Ireland chasing James for as long as possible. In fact, refugees who made their way to William's camp reported that the French had been ordered by Louvois to act on the defensive and not to risk a battle. George Story heard from such refugees that the plan was to fight delaying actions from Newry southward to the Boyne in the hope that there would be an insurrection in England or that the French navy would be strong enough to intervene. Therefore, Lauzun had strongly opposed James' resolve to fight and had won Lord Tyrconnell to his way of thinking. But Lauzun's military experience was negligible and, although James himself admitted that he came to a 'resolution of avoiding a battle all he could', he realised that his men were becoming dispirited and that, if he abandoned the positions on the Boyne, he would lose most of the province of Leinster and possibly Munster and his army would then become considerably weakened by desertion.

A Jacobite colonel, Charles O'Kelly, of Aughrane, Co. Galway, referring to James' retreat from Dundalk to the Boyne, recalled that 'the Irish army was not a little disheartened by this sudden retreat of James: for as nothing animates the Irish more than to be led out to assault, so nothing can discourage them more than to retire from an enemy. And this is common to all new raised troops, but particularly to such as are not so well officered, which was too much the case here; for Tyrconnell employed very few but creatures of his own, though never so unfit to command.'

Colonel O'Kelly was not actually with the Jacobite army. This seventy-nine-year-old officer, who had studied in Belgium and fought for the Royalists during the Civil War, was stationed in Galway. A member of the Irish Parliament for Roscommon and of James' Privy Council, he commanded a Jacobite regiment safeguarding Galway from Williamite attack. His information came from his son Captain Denis O'Kelly who was serving in Lord Galmoy's regiment of horse. Three years before his death in 1695, Colonel O'Kelly wrote a volume which he entitled *Macarie Excidium, or the Destruction of Cyprus* in which he recounted the history of the war but disguised all the names and places with classical allusions as if he were writing about Cyprus.

James, writing to his wife Mary of Modena some twenty days later, explained 'that he was well aware he should be blamed for having risked an action on such unequal terms; but that, if it were to be risked, there was not any situation more favourable; and if he had continued always retreating, he would have lost all without striking a stroke, and have been driven fairly into the sea.'

The Comte de Lauzun, in a despatch to the Marquis de Seignelay, said he thought it was impossible to put up a resistance on the Boyne. The day he reached the Boyne, he claimed, he had reconnoitred upstream as far as Slane and found the river fordable 'everywhere'. His compatriot, the Marquis Lery de Girardin, commanding the French cavalry, disagreed with Lauzun. He later stated that the site was a good one and the most advantageous position for a battle that could have been selected between Dundalk and Dublin. He felt that night that the prospects for a Jacobite victory on July 1 were very favourable. James certainly agreed. 'This appeared', he recalled, 'to him to be a tolerable good post, and the best in the country. He therefore resolved to continue there, and wait for the enemy, although his army did not amount to more than twenty thousand men, and that of the Prince of Orange to between forty and fifty thousand.'

The decision to stand and fight delighted the young Duke of Berwick, who noted: 'The enemy had five and forty thousand men and we were only three and twenty thousand. This great disproportion determined us to attempt seizing some post by which we might stop the progress of the Prince of Orange or at least give him battle with less advantage.' The position at the Boyne, he felt, was just such a post. Burnet, recalling the opposition of Lauzun, was to write some fifteen years later: 'In opposition to all this opinion King James himself was positive that they must stay and defend the Boyne; if they marched off and abandoned Dublin, they would lose their reputation, that the people would leave them and capitulate, it would also disperse all their friends in England. Therefore he resolved to maintain the post he was in, and seemed not a little pleased to think that he should have one fair battle for his crown.'

James was very explicit in his reason for standing at the Boyne. 'The reason that induced the King to risk such an action with such unequal numbers', he wrote in his *Memoirs*, 'was his feeling that otherwise he should be obliged to abandon Dublin and all Munster without striking a stroke and to retire behind the River Shannon in Connaught, a province the least fertile in grain of all Ireland, and in which, as he had no magazine, he could not subsist long. Besides, his troops were impatient for a battle and being new recruits would have been greatly discouraged by a continued retreat, and if they had taken a disgust would probably have dispersed or at least would have murmured at the little confidence reposed in them by the King. . . .'

Colonel O'Kelly, while recognising the dangers of demoralisation if James continued his retreat, nevertheless supported Lauzun that the Jacobite army should not have come to grips with the Williamites until they were absolutely forced to. He wrote:

But we must confess that the measures taken all along by James were in no way agreeable to the rules of true prudence and good politics, or to the ancient and modern maxims of war, for, as it is a received principle among conquerors to hasten the decision of the quarrel by battle whilst their army is fresh, hearty and numerous, so it is the known interest of those who are on the defensive to follow contrary methods and so delay coming to a general engagement until the invaders may be had at a cheap rate, when fatigues, disease and other incommodities, which they are to expect in an enemy's country, will make them notably decay, both in courage and number, and when they are so harassed that they may be easily defeated without any great hazard. Besides, a victory which is obtained without bloodshed and loss of men, brings more reputation to the general, for it is wholly attributed to his own conduct; whereas his captains and soldiers must share with him in the glory of gaining a battle. It was therefore the interest of James not to fight at that time, but to retire to Dublin and join the rest of his troops left for the guard of that city, where he might have three parts of the kingdom at his back to furnish him with the necessaries.

The anonymous author of the Jacobite account, *Light to the Blind*, thought to be a lawyer named Nicholas Plunkett, did not agree with James' position in the first place and also felt that he had not defended it to the best advantage.

If the King resolved to stand his ground, why did he not use the common rules of art military for the strengthening of an inferior army against a superior? By which means the inferior doth gain often the point, as we shall see in the experience of wars. There was at that time but a few narrow passages to be fortified on the Boyne which might have been done in the space of three hours by three hundred pioneers.

Light to the Blind maintains that if James had dug entrenchments and William had then decided to march to Navan to seek a crossing, James could then have followed him, 'having the more expeditious army and might have entrenched there in the like manner'. But the Williamites had observed that Oldbridge was loopholed and that breastworks had been thrown up along the river together with the fences of the fields which supplied adequate cover for defending the Jacobite positions. Therefore more entrenchments were surely not needed? The author of *Light to the Blind* continues, however, to say:

. . . by these obstructions given to the enemy's passage, [James] could have called to his succour 18,000 resolute men of the Catholic militia and volunteers out of the adjacent counties of Meath, Dublin and Kildare, some armed with swords, some with half pikes, some with firearms, and some with scythes, which with skilful management would likely turn the balance to the King's side, considering how propense the people were at that time to fight against a most odious enemy who came to devour their all. But unfortunately none of these courses were taken, which makes me fear that some one or more of the King's counsellors were underhand and intent upon the destruction of the nation. Otherwise, how is it possible that such gross errors should be committed in the government of the army, and in using right ways and means against the attempt of the enemy?

The simple truth was that the Jacobites were taken in by William's superior strategy. The author of *Light to the Blind* certainly did not seem to be in touch with the reality of the situation and, at one point, he maintains that James had decided to break camp and march his army to the west on the morning of July 1. During the evening of June 30, however, James had decided to send the baggage of the army south towards Duleek in preparation for the battle, and the soldiers were told to wear a white cockade, in deference to their French allies, as their badge of distinction.

James expected the main thrust of William's army to come across the fords along the Oldbridge sector. His men had destroyed the bridge at Slane and Lord Iveagh, in Drogheda, guarded the only other bridge, thereby protecting the flanks of the army. But Lieutenant-General Richard Hamilton had pointed out to James the dangers of the ford at Rosnaree. Lauzun says that Neil O'Neill's dragoon regiment was posted at Slane Bridge on June 29 with orders to send out scouting parties in case the Williamites marched upstream to try to ford there or at Rosnaree. James says that O'Neill was not posted there until June 30 and this was done presumably at the instigation of Hamilton. O'Neill had been ordered to defend the Slane and Rosnaree areas as long as he could without being cut to pieces, but the very fact that only one dragoon regiment was placed in this area showed James' confidence that Oldbridge would be the main centre of attack. James considered that any crossing on the Jacobite left flank would only be a diversionary attack on that flank or a Williamite attempt to race for Dublin and capture the capital.

Lauzun was to write that he reported to James on the night of the 30th that the Williamites were extending their right flank towards Slane. As the Williamite movement did not begin until after 6 a.m. it must have been soon after this that the excited French commander informed James that most of the enemy were heading for the Slane crossing. Marquis de la Hoguette, Lauzun's maréchal de camp, recalled that in the early hours of July 1 a hurried council of war decided to move the main Jacobite positions to the left to face the enemy crossing from the direction of Slane and Rosnaree at daybreak.

CHAPTER 2

JULY 1, 1690

'they went down briskly'

Captain Rowland Davies, the chaplain of Lord Cavendish's regiment of horse, was roused from his sleep at two o'clock to find the camp being awakened by the long roll of the General Call to Arms. The left-handed drag and quick beat of the right on the drums made a thunderous and remorseless sound. The night was cold, extremely cold for a summer's night, even in Ireland. The extreme heat of the day and the coldness of the night had caused a dense mist to lay close to the ground, making it difficult for the yawning cavalrymen to saddle their horses and form themselves into orderly troops. Cavendish's horse was one of the first regiments to awaken and prepare itself. Now it had to stand to, each man holding his horse's head, while the other regiments of cavalry, dragoons and foot, cursing and stumbling in the darkness and the mist, made ready.

Although the sun was supposed to rise at five o'clock that morning, the thick mist shrouded everything as effectively as if it had still been dark. It was not until about five or six o'clock that Count Meinhard Schomberg was able to give the order for his division of near eight thousand men to march off through the woods in the direction of Slane, passing Townley Hall before joining the main Drogheda to Slane road by the hamlet of Monknewtown. The mist was a godsend to Meinhard Schomberg who was perhaps not in the best of spirits having only hours before celebrated his forty-ninth birthday with his father and his fellow officers. He, like his father, enjoyed a drink—unlike their austere king—and perhaps if he snapped his orders to his aide-de-camp, St. Felix, he was to be forgiven. The Jacobite camp must already know that they were on the move. Indeed, James recalled in his *Memoirs*, 'we heard the general beat before day in the enemy's camp'. But thanks to the mist the Jacobites could not see the extent of the flanking movement to the right of William's army. The impression that Count Schomberg wanted to give was that his force constituted the main body of the Williamites, but not until he was ready to do so, and he was therefore grateful for the mist.

The Count's division consisted of 4,000 horse and two dragoon regiments, one of which was Colonel Eppinger's Dutch dragoons. Behind these men, their breaths puffing in the cold morning air, came 3,000 foot soldiers under the command of the English Brigadier Trelawney, who also had with him five small field guns. The cavalry included the French regiment of Count Schomberg's own command in which, as there seemed no other French cavalry in the area, the French cavalry trooper Gideon Bonnivert must have been serving. Bonnivert recalls being up at two o'clock that morning and marching off about five, although Rowland Davies noted that it was six o'clock before his regiment moved off.

Having crossed the Mattock River and reached Monknew-town, Count Schomberg detached a small body of horse and sent it galloping along the two and a half miles to the town of Slane. Although Captain Pownel had already reported the bridge to be destroyed, Count Schomberg was a careful general, like his father, and decided to check it for himself. Slane was a vantage point not to be ignored. In Norman times it had been a considerable town and the famous Hill of Slane was where St. Patrick was reported to have lit the Paschal Fire on the Eve of Easter A.D. 433 in defiance of the druids. An Augustinian Abbey had been founded there in 1190, attracting scholars from many parts of Europe, and had later been refounded as a Franciscan Abbey by one Christopher Fleming in 1512. Count Schomberg was not interested in history but an abbey was a building which could be fortified and he did not want a hostile garrison to attack his rear. So he despatched cavalry troops to reconnoitre the town as he swung off the main road towards the small group of stone houses that lay on the south side of the Boyne at Rosnaree.

Count Schomberg's division marched across the fields, through woods, across the old Bronze Age tumulus of New-grange, which, with that of Knowth and Dowth, consisted of the Brugh na Bóinne, the palace of the Boyne, which the Irish revered in their ancient literature. Newgrange particularly they revered, Caiseal Aonghasa, as the Irish called it, with its surrounding standing stones which must have called forth more than passing comment from the marching soldiers. In reality the tumuli were royal tombs of the ancient pre-Christian Celtic society. Bodies of chieftains lay in their domed chambers. But to the Irish they were the dwelling places of the gods and one god in particular, Aonghasa or Angus, as the name was Anglicised. Aonghasa was a young god, a beautiful youth who lived at Caiseal Aonghasa adorned in flowers. Brugh na Bóinne had belonged originally to Elchmhaire the divine, Aonghasa's foster father. Aonghasa's real father was Daghdha, chief of the gods, who had an illicit union with Boann, wife of Nechtan, a water god, who gave his name to the great river of Irish mythology. Daghdha and Boann caused the sun to stand still for nine months so that Aonghasa was conceived and born on the same day. Aonghasa did not have a happy relationship with his foster father and one day Manannán Mac Lir, the god of the sea, suggested to Aonghasa how he could take possession of the Brugh na Bóinne. This Aonghasa did and remained there drinking the ale of immortality surrounded by an invisible wall. As the god of love, Aonghasa was susceptible to love himself and fell in love with Édáin, wife of Midhir. When Édáin was separated from Midhir through the evil magic of his first wife Fuanmhnach, Aonghasa placed her in a grianán, a sunny chamber of crystal big enough to carry with him. Fuamhnach intervened and Aonghasa lost her. But the intrepid lover set out to search Ireland for a girl he had dreamed about and finally found her. Together, in the shape of swans, the lovers flew back to Brugh na Bóinne and lived there chanting such wondrous music that all who heard it slept for three days and nights.

But there was no beautiful music to lull Count Schomberg's men to sleep as they sweated and cursed their way past Aonghasa's resting place. It was nearly eight o'clock now, as the soldiers came within sight of the ford that led across to Rosnaree. The river was extremely shallow in this place and completely unaffected by the tidal currents. Gideon Bonnivert remembered coming down a very steep hill to find a shallow river at the bottom of it. 'That led into a very fine plain: as we came there we found a party of the enemy with four or five pieces of artillery ready to receive us, but that did not daunt our men. They went down briskly notwithstanding the continual fire upon us.'

According to the Count's aide-de-camp, St. Felix, writing to
Countess Schomberg on the following day, Count Schomberg's
division marched five miles to the ford, which, he said, was
guarded by 1,200 horse. He had mistaken a Jacobite dragoon
regiment for cavalry and instead of 1,200 men disputing the
passage of Schomberg's 10,000 there were only 480 men with
three small field guns, the entire eight troops of Sir Neil
O'Neill's dragoons. It was more by luck than good management that O'Neill's entire force was concentrated around the
Rosnaree ford. O'Neill of Killelagh in Kilutagh, who had been
created a baronet in 1666 and raised his regiment at his own
expense, had been ordered to Slane by the Jacobite commander
of the area, the French Marquis Lery de Girardin. But O'Neill
had found that the bridge had already been destroyed and the
river was fairly impassable there. Besides, he had reasoned to
his second-in-command, Henry O'Neill, what was the use of
guarding Slane when the Williamites could easily ford the river
at Rosnaree? So it was that at eight o'clock, as the mist began
to clear and the sun shine fiercely on what promised to be the
hottest day yet of that summer, Sir Neil O'Neill's 480 men
stood facing the first Williamite attack of 10,000 seasoned
troopers. The Jacobite commander immediately brought up his
three field pieces and began to pour a steady stream of fire
from his dismounted men towards the crossing which was a
fairly narrow one.

Count Schomberg sent one hundred of his toughest grenadiers across the river to draw O'Neill's fire and judge what
opposition he had to contend with. Then he ordered Eppinger's
Dutch dragoons across. According to Bonnivert, 'the grenadiers
and dragoons were first on the other side and we soon followed
them'. As Eppinger's Dutch dragoons splashed their horses
across the river, O'Neill mounted his men and charged them.
St. Felix wrote: 'The enemy charged but the Count observed
the enemy were in disorder. Sword in hand he led his dragoons
through the river. He charged them so effectually that they
were driven two miles back. The infantry were left to cross as
best they could.' The breaking of the Jacobite dragoons had
been occasioned by O'Neill receiving a wound in the thigh and
several of his officers and men falling. O'Neill was taken from
the field by his dragoons bleeding profusely from a wound from
which he was to die eight days later in Waterford. James

declared in his *Memoirs* that 'Sir Neil O'Neill's dragoons did
their part well, and disputed the passage with the enemy almost
an hour till their cannon came up and then retired in good
order with the loss of only five or six common men but the
colonel shot through the thigh and an officer or two wounded'.
James was badly informed because O'Neill's dragoons left fifty
of their comrades dead on the field before falling back.

Count Schomberg had firmly secured the first Williamite
bridgehead across the Boyne by 9.30 a.m. with comparatively
little loss of life. The only casualty of any note among his
officers was Isaac de Prepetit, quarter master of Count Schomberg's French cavalry, who was badly wounded. St. Felix was
immediately despatched back to William's general staff headquarters to inform them of the situation. He reached William,
having ridden hard, at the same time that Count Schomberg
was consolidating on the south bank. William was delighted by
the news and ordered Lieutenant-General Douglas to march
after Count Schomberg with a reinforcement of a cavalry
brigade.

As soon as the Marquis Lery de Girardin heard of the
Williamite attack on O'Neill's position he sent messages to
his immediate commander, the Comte de Lauzun, and told
him that the Williamites had passed the river 'below Slane'.
Lauzun now fell into William's trap by informing James that
the Williamites were making their major attack on the Jacobite
left flank. Lauzun began to march towards Rosnaree taking the
most experienced troops the Jacobites possessed, the 'French'
regiments of Conrad von Zurlauben, Biron, Bouilly, Tirlon and
Chémerault, with six of the Jacobite six-pounder field guns.
James thought that the Williamite attack was 'as if they intended to take us in the flank or get between us and Dublin'.
James now gave orders that the greater part of the army was
to follow Lauzun, 'taking it for granted that the main body of
the enemy would follow their right wing'.

The village of Oldbridge was now defended by two infantry
regiments of the Earls of Clanricarde and Antrim. These were
reinforced by a battery of field guns, one to the south of Oldbridge and the other opposite Yellow Island. Several regiments
were withdrawn to face the threat on the left flank. De la
Hoguette commented: 'Oldbridge was held by only one battalion. Two French battalions and another Irish battalion, which

had been placed there the previous evening, were withdrawn early in the morning.' De la Hoguette was misinformed on the number of troops that were in Oldbridge later that morning but the comment underlines the point that James withdrew a large number of men as soon as he heard of the attack at Rosnaree. In fact, he rode down to Oldbridge to converse with Tyrconnell about the numbers he required. Tyrconnell demanded that James leave him sufficient men to defend Oldbridge in case of attack. He was left with a total of seven infantry regiments, three cavalry regiments and two troops of King James' Horse Guards, a total of 5,500 men, who shortly would have to face William's main attack of 15,000 troops. James had also withdrawn a reserve brigade that had been positioned behind the hill of Donore, under the command of Sir Charles Carney, which consisted of Nicholas Purcell's regiment of horse and Nicholas Browne's foot regiment. Another brigade of infantry commanded by the veteran of Killiecrankie and Derry, Major-General John Wauchope, was also moved from the Old-bridge area. Wauchope, according to Colonel O'Kelly, 'was a Scotsman by birth, but zealous enough for the Roman Catholic religion and also seemed no less concerned for the Irish interest'. Among the regiments in Wauchope's brigade was that of the Grand Prior in which Captain John Stevens was serving. Stevens says the report ran through the regiment that Slane was in the hands of the enemy and the order was given to join the Comte de Lauzun. The mist had now entirely evaporated and the movements on the opposite bank could be seen. Lieutenant-General Douglas' division was observed moving off towards Monknewtown, between the hills. 'And now we saw them,' wrote Stevens, 'marching off from the right towards it [Slane]. We on the other side [of the Boyne] marched from the left, the river being between both; for a considerable space we marched under the enemy's cannon, which they played furiously without any intermission yet did but little execution.'

The reinforcements marched south along the river, past the old farm lying on its banks a mile from Oldbridge. Then, moving away from the river, and away from the Williamite batteries, the Jacobites skirted the three hundred feet high hill by the small cluster of deserted crofts called Stallen and, leaving the village of Donore to their left, joined the main road to Duleek. At the crossroads, less than a mile from Donore, where the road divided to Slane, the command was given to leave the roadway and climb across some low hills due west. For two-and-a-half miles the main body of the Jacobite army sweated its way across the small but sharply rising and falling hillocks.

In the meantime, James and the major part of his cavalry and dragoons, with Major-Generals Patrick Sarsfield, Thomas Maxwell, Anthony and John Hamilton, and Alexander Rainier, the Marquis de Boisseleau, had joined Lauzun and the Marquis Lery de Girardin. The Jacobites had taken up a position straddling the Rosnaree to Duleek road about one-and-three-quarter miles from the ford at Rosnaree. Without realising it, Lauzun had taken up a position south-east of a fairly substantial bog, a mile north of the bog of Gillestown, and his whole front was therefore protected by it and a riverlet that ran south from the Boyne into the bog.

Count Schomberg, equally unknowingly in spite of his guides from the Enniskillen regiments, marched the main bulk of his division into the bog itself. He was heavily reinforced by Douglas' division which crossed the Boyne in three columns at Rosnaree and another ford a quarter of a mile towards Slane and at Slane itself. Richard Brewer of Lord Lisburn's colonial foot regiment wrote: 'There were two brigades of us that for want of knowing the ground marched through such a bog that I thought the Devil himself could not have got through and so did the enemy or they had not faced us as they did for half an hour almost within musket shot. But . . . a prisoner told me that as soon as they saw us get over the bog, it half broke their hearts. For my part, I thought I should never have got out of it.'

The truth was that the Jacobites did not know of the existence of the bog either. Captain Rowland Davies recalled: 'We saw the enemy making towards us and that they drew up on the side of a hill in two lines, the river on their right.' As chance would have it Lauzun had positioned his men where a deep, narrow gorge cut along from the river Boyne, along the path of the riverlet into a steep boggy valley which presented a considerable obstacle between the two forces. Lord Meath, who commanded his colonial foot regiment in Count Schomberg's division, wrote in a disgruntled fashion four days later to a lady friend in England: 'We drew up to enclose the enemy's whole army but a damn deep bog lay between us: we could not soon pass it, which gave them time to run for it.'

The entire manoeuvre had lasted several hours. From the time of the securing of the bridgehead at Rosnaree to the deployment of the Jacobite left wing, or rather the main body, between Rosnaree and Duleek, some three to four hours had passed. James' general staff were now pressing for the engagement to commence but the full body of the Jacobite infantry had not come up, for they were still struggling across the hills to Lauzun's position. Thus James 'did not think proper to begin the attack yet, because he was waiting for the troops he had left at Oldbridge'.

It was just after two o'clock that a red-faced aide-de-camp galloped up to the group of generals, waiting impatiently for the arrival of the rest of their infantry. The news he told directly to James in a horrified whisper. William's main force had smashed their way across the ford at Oldbridge and another force had crossed at Drybridge, a little further towards Drogheda—the Jacobites were fleeing in disorder towards Duleek. 'The enemy had forced the pass at Oldbridge', said the aide-de-camp, 'and the right wing was beaten.'

'my poor guards, my poor guards, my poor guards'

The dense mist had dispersed from the valleys around the Williamite camp by eight o'clock and the sun had risen in a cloudless sky. According to Story, 'the day was very clear as if the sun itself had a mind to see what would happen'. Shortly afterwards the Williamite artillery started to pound the Jacobite positions in Oldbridge. William's Secretary at War in Ireland, George Clarke, observed that 'about eight or nine our cannon began to fire upon two houses with yards walled about, that stood on each side [of] the road on the other side [of] the Boyne, just over against the ford where the Guards were to pass'. Clarke was a keen observer of the battle. His father, Sir William, had been Secretary at War to the Commonwealth and later served Charles II in the same capacity, dying of his wounds in the sea battle of Harwich in June 1666. His son, feeling his father's death closely, had shunned the military way of life and became an academic. He entered Brasenose, Oxford, in 1679 and obtained several degrees, finally becoming a Fellow of All Souls. In 1685 he plunged into the political world as a Tory and was elected to the House of Commons. Famed for the courtliness of his manner and architectural taste, Clarke had held office as Judge Advocate-General, had been secretary to Prince Georg of Daamstadt and was now William's Secretary at War. But according to one contemporary, 'Clarke is a pitiful proud sneaker and an enemy to true loyalty'. Clarke was not the only member of William's government in Ireland to comment on the battle. Sir Robert Southwell, the Secretary of State for Ireland, found time to sit down and write a letter while the cannonade was taking place, observing that Count Schomberg had succeeded in crossing the river at the upper fords and that the attack on Oldbridge was about to begin. The idea, he suggests, was for William and Count Schomberg to encircle the Jacobite army in a pincer movement 'expecting that all may soon be disordered on the other side when both parties meet'.

William's aide-de-camp, Sir Thomas Bellingham, was up early and had been asked by Major-General Percy Kirk to see if he could discover any information on the state of the Jacobite army. He 'brought in a youth, one Fyans, who came that morning from Drogheda. I carried him to the King who was standing at the battery seeing his cannon play at the house of Oldbridge'. There was little the youth Fyans could add to the knowledge William already had about his adversaries. The author of *Villare Hibernicum* comments: 'We understood by a Protestant deserter that swam over the river last night that the enemy was 25,000 strong, that they had sent away some of their heaviest baggage, as they gave out, to fight us.'

William, according to reports, had rested very well that night, had risen early and, by eight o'clock, was on horseback making preparations for the assault. He was wearing full decorations, including his Star and Garter, which made him a conspicuous target to the enemy, observed Southwell. In addition, his wound troubled him so that he was unable to wear his cuirass, the defensive breastplate and backplate, which made him more vulnerable. Soon after nine o'clock Count Schomberg's aide-de-camp, St. Felix, had arrived with the news of the fording of Rosnaree and Douglas had been despatched with reinforcements. The Williamite artillery had cannonaded Oldbridge for long enough to demoralise the Jacobite infantry dug in there and it was now low tide on the river. The time had come to make the first assault.

On the northern slopes of the hill of Donore 'Fighting Dick Talbot', Lord Tyrconnell, the 'ass' of Wharton's famous *Lillebulero*, who had, according to one Dubliner, reduced Ireland 'from a place of briskest trade and the best paid rent in Christendom to ruin and desolation', sat uneasily surveying the build-up of William's forces through a field glass. Little trace was left of the flamboyant lover and duelist who had been left for dead when Cromwell had massacred the inhabitants of Drogheda, afterwards escaping to Spain to be a scourge to the Protectorate. Now, Richard Talbot, Earl of Tyrconnell, whom James had raised to dukedom on his landing at Kinsale, was an old man of sixty. According to Berwick's estimation, 'he had not a military genius but much courage'. But it did not take military genius to feel some unease at the developing situation, for if William chose to launch his main attack on Oldbridge, Tyrconnell knew he did not have enough troops to repulse him.

Richard Talbot was descended from the Norman de Talbots to whom Henry II granted estates at Malahide in 1174. They were a family who had 'sunk into degeneracy which had adopted the manners of the Celts'. Richard was the youngest son of Sir William Talbot and Alison Netterville. His eldest brother Sir Robert had been one of the leaders of the Irish Confederate Parliament of 1642 but Richard had fought against Eoin Ruadh O'Neill and the Confederates and later against the Parliamentarians in the shaky Confederate-Royalist alliance. Another elder brother, Peter, was Catholic archbishop of Dublin; he had died in prison in 1680. As Charles II lay dying Richard Talbot was given command of the army in Ireland and three months after the accession of James was created Earl of Tyrconnell. Tyrconnell disbanded all Protestant militia and started to Catholicise the country. For a time he served James II in England as an adviser but returned in June 1686, as Lord General, becoming Lord Deputy the following January. His politics were clear. He wanted to restore the estates of the Catholic Old English in Ireland of which the Cromwellian settlement had deprived them. He told Lord Clarendon, the viceroy in Ireland: 'By God, my lords, these Acts of Settlement and this new interest are damned things; we do know all those arts and damned roguish contrivances which procured those acts.' And now the future of those Acts of Settlement was about to be put to the test for all time.

On the sloping ground behind Oldbridge Tyrconnell had drawn up his own regiment of horse, some two hundred men, with Colonel Hugh Sutherland's regiment and Colonel John Parker's regiment. In addition to these three cavalry regiments there were two troops of the King's Horse Guards under the overall command of the young Duke of Berwick. Under Berwick's command, and commanding the first troop of the Horse Guards, some two hundred troopers, was Henry Jermyn, Viscount Dover. Of all the Jacobite commanders Lord Dover was the least happy with his lot. He had done his utmost to avoid engaging further in the war. Eleven days ago, on June 19, he had written to the Williamite Major-General Percy Kirk: 'You will be much surprised to receive a letter from me but, after the many revolutions we have seen in our time, nothing is to be wondered at.' He had begged Kirk to use his influence with the Duke of Schomberg 'to obtain a pass for my Lady Dover, myself, and the little vessel we shall go in, and those few servants specified in the written note, to go and stay in Ostend, till such time as I may otherwise dispose myself'. Dover was sick of the political situation. At fifty-four years of age, he wanted a more settled family life. He had served James II well, he felt, and had organised the flight of James, the little Prince of Wales, to France before joining James in Ireland. And the Irish had shown damned little affection for him. James' French adviser, Jean-Antoine de Mesmes, Comte d'Avaux, had said of him: 'He appears to be much estranged from the nation and he is not more liked by the Irish, having expressed himself more than once to their disadvantage'. So, felt Dover, it was time to quit Ireland and James, but he had received no word from the Williamites since his note to Kirk and now he was involved in a battle. Henry Jermyn was not happy in his thoughts.

As reserves, Tyrconnell had two dragoon regiments, those of Lord Walter Dongan, 'a high spirited young man' who was the son of the Earl of Limerick, and the regiment of Daniel O'Brien, the third Viscount Clare, who was a member of James' Privy Council and lord-lieutenant of Co. Clare. Both dragoon regiments consisted of eight troops of fifty men, making four hundred men at full strength. The total strength of the cavalry facing William was 1,500 men plus 800 dragoons. As for infantry, apart from the two regiments in Oldbridge, Tyrconnell had five more regiments in reserve making a total foot strength of 4,000 men.

Tyrconnell's general staff shared his uneasiness. Lieutenant-General Richard Hamilton, whom Tyrconnell had placed in overall command of the foot at Oldbridge, had seen his fears of an attack at Slane or Rosnaree realised. Now he wondered whether James had interpreted the attack correctly. Was it the main attack or merely a feint? Richard Hamilton was one of the most popular Jacobite generals, the fifth son of Sir George Hamilton of Dunalong, a younger son of Lord Abercorn, and a cousin to Gustavus Hamilton, the governor of Enniskillen who had conducted the town's defences against the Jacobites and was even now waiting to lead his Enniskillen Foot across the Oldbridge ford. Richard Hamilton had been admired because he 'zealously protected the Protestants' during his operations in Ulster the previous year.

Another commander who shared Tyrconnell's fears was Lieutenant-General of Horse Dominic Sheldon, in overall command of the cavalry. He was, according to O'Kelly, 'an Englishman by birth of the Roman Catholic religion, brought into Ireland on the accession of James the Second by Tyrconnell and by him made captain of a company of men-at-arms'. The only other general staff officer in the area was Brigadier William Dorrington who was in command of the Royal Regiment of Foot, which, at full strength, was composed of twenty-two companies of ninety men per company. 'All,' according to Captain Stevens, 'well armed, clad in red lined with blue, their colours the royal colours of England, St. George's Cross and the arms of the four kingdoms.' The Royal Regiment was one of Tyrconnell's five reserve infantry regiments. Also among the foot was a regiment of raw Irish recruits commanded by the French Marquis d'Hoquincourt.

Among the few stone houses that comprised the village of Oldbridge, now deserted by their inhabitants who had fled to Drogheda for safety, the soldiers of the infantry regiments of the Earl of Clanricarde and Antrim sheltered themselves as best they could from William's cannonade. Great holes had been blown in the walls of the houses and part of the little church tower had been smashed by the six-pound cannon balls and the heavier missiles from the howitzers.

Alexander MacDonnell, the elderly third earl of Antrim, was not new to this form of fighting. He had begun a military career as the commander of a regiment raised to defend the Irish Catholic Confederacy in 1642 and from 1649 to 1651 he had fought the Cromwellians under the military-bishop Emer MacMahon. Finally forced to surrender, he was allowed to take his men to France to serve in the French army. His estates were forfeit and when his elder brother Randal died in 1683 he had succeeded to an impoverished earldom. With the hope for restitution of his estates springing up he had raised a regiment for James and made an attempt to seize Derry which had sparked off the famous siege. At full strength Lord Antrim had 650 men under his command, all fitted out in white jackets and knee breeches, lined with red. The flag of the regiment fluttered over Oldbridge—a red cross on a green field, in each quarter of the field a hand emerging from the clouds holding a cross of Jerusalem, while in the centre was an Irish harp surmounted by a crown imperial with the motto *in hoc signo vinces*—by this sign we win.

Now the cluster of general officers round Tyrconnell could see a movement on the opposite bank, could hear the ominous crash of sticks upon drum skins and could see the Williamite lines beginning to move towards the ford. Tyrconnell immediately ordered Brigadier Dorrington into Oldbridge with the Royal Regiment to support Antrim and Clanricarde and also ordered the rest of his infantry to take up positions along the south bank of the river to the east of Oldbridge.

Bellingham records that the attack on Oldbridge commenced about 11 a.m. He was writing his account later that evening. But George Story contradicts him by stating the attack began about fifteen minutes after ten o'clock and in this he is supported by the Danish ambassador, M. de la Fouleresse. Story did not, of course, know that William had received news of Count Schomberg's successful crossing from St. Felix because, he says: '. . . the King . . . computed the time when he thought our right wing was over and then he ordered the foot to attack the pass at Oldbridge.'

The first regiment into the attack were the three battalions of William's corps d'élite, the Dutch Blue Guards. The first honour of the battle went to Heinrich Maastrict Solms, the Count of Solms-Braunfels, who had led these same three battalions up the Mall in London, colours flying, drums beating and matches lighted, to occupy Whitehall for William. Now, as easy in his saddle as he had been when he rode up the Mall, the Count gave the order for the colours to be raised, the drums and fifes struck up a march and the Dutch Guards, clad in the dark blue jackets and knee breeches, began to march towards the river. The English officers of William's army could not help betraying some of their annoyance. They agreed the Count was a capable divisional leader, brave to a fault, but his arrogance and rude incomprehensible behaviour had made him one of the most detested of William's soldiers.

The march that the fifes and drums of the Dutch Blue Guards chose to play was the ever popular *Lillebulero*. The jaunty strains of the music must have rankled in the ears of the Irish Jacobites as it carried across the river.

As the Guards reached the river's edge, Solms-Braunfels and his staff drew their horses to the side and straight, without falter, as if on a parade ground, the fifes and drums not missing a note, the Dutch marched past into the river. Story recalled: 'the Dutch beat a march till they got to the river's side, and then the drums ceasing, in they went, some eight or ten abreast. . . .' The crossing was made a few yards to the west of Grove Island, the Dutch going in up to their waists, holding their new snaphaunce muskets over their heads. The Danish ambassador wrote to his King, Christian V, the next day: 'The regiment of the Dutch Guards was the first to cross, the men being above their waists in water. The enemy occupied a village on the bank, about which there are small gardens enclosed by hedges.' The strength of the Dutch Guards, 1,931 strong, was almost equivalent to that of the Jacobite troops in Oldbridge.

The Jacobite infantry waited until the Dutch were half-way across when, according to Story, 'a whole peal of shot came from the hedges, breastworks and houses'. In the main, the fire was fairly ineffectual. The Jacobite infantry had fired high. But the first casualty of the crossing was a lieutenant of the Dutch grenadier company, an obvious target in his uniform of piebald, yellow and red, with his fur-lined cap. The lieutenant had been trying to form up the leading files, crouching so that his men could fire over his head. To throw the Dutch grenadier

companies against the Jacobite positions first was a good strategic move of Solms-Braunfels, for these were the shock troops
and a new form of fighting soldier not seen in Ireland before.
Each grenadier carried three grenades, each weighing three
pounds, in his pouch. They could light the fuses and throw
them into the enemy at close range, causing great devastation.

In spite of the volley fire from the Jacobite positions the
Dutch Guards began to struggle ashore on the south bank.
Their numbers were so great in the river that they had caused
the tide to effectually stop and the river to dam. Major Arthur
Ashton, leading the first battalion of the Jacobite Royal Regiment of Foot, led his troops to the water's edge. Seizing a pike
from a trooper he ran it through an officer of the Dutch Guards
as the man tried to scramble up the bank, but a guardsman
following the officer shot the major who died later of the wound.
'The Jacobite resistance to the Dutch was strong', observed
Story, 'the fighting was so hot that many old soldiers said they
never saw brisker work.'

After a while the Dutch managed to push the Jacobites away
from the river and slowly back out of Oldbridge, house by house
and wall by wall. The Danish ambassador was perhaps a little
too carried away by the success when he reported to Christian V
the next day that 'the Dutch rushed to the attack with such
impetus that their opponents immediately abandoned their
positions and our men, having pursued them for some time,
drew themselves up in battle formation to maintain the ground
they had gained'.

The Dutch Guards had, unaided, forced the Jacobite infantry
back from the river with a loss of only 150 men. They continued
their push until the Royal Regiment had been dislodged from
Oldbridge and then they formed up with military precision to
await reinforcements. William decided to commit the colonial
regiments, Gustavus Hamilton's Enniskilleners and the contingents from Derry and Newtownbutler. These were to march
across the river in the wake of the Dutch Guards while the two
Huguenot regiments of Cambron and Caillimote were to cross
over Grove Island together with the English foot regiments of
Colonel Sir John Hanmer and Colonel St. John. These were to
be backed by the 652 men of the Dutch foot regiment of Count
Henry Nassau, Lord Auverquerque, who seems to have left his
joint command of the reserve entirely to Bentinck and to have

persuaded William, his cousin, to use him in the forward troops. The forty-nine-year-old Auverquerque cut a resplendent figure, carrying a gold hilted sword, gold inlaid pistols and a pair of gold horse buckles that the Dutch States-General had presented to him after he had saved William's life at the battle of Mons on August 13, 1678. Auverquerque was the third son of Louis, Count Nassau, illegitimate son of Maurice, Prince of Orange, and great uncle of William. His cousin had rewarded him for his faithful service by making him master of his horse and Parliament had conferred English naturalisation on him in 1689.

As Tyrconnell saw these regiments marching to their crossing points he realised that it was time to commit his cavalry to try to drive the Dutch back across the river. He ordered Berwick to lead both troops of Horse Guards, with Parker and Sutherland in support, against the Dutch now formed up in lines before Oldbridge. Richard Hamilton was to form up the foot and, with Lord Antrim's regiment to protect his flank from the Dutch, he was to meet the Williamite regiments now beginning to cross over Grove Island.

The Jacobite cavalry swung round the hill of Donore towards the Dutch Guards halted before Oldbridge. Story observed: 'One would have thought that men and horses had risen out of the earth for now there appeared a great many battalions and squadrons of the enemy, all of a sudden, who stood behind the little hills.' According to the Danish ambassador, 'a moment later, three squadrons of King James' bodyguard, which appeared to be very determined, rushed sword in hand upon this regiment, to whose support a regiment of French refugees and some English regiments were hurrying.'

Without any sign of alarm the Dutch Blue Guards formed squares to counter the cavalry charge of nearly one thousand men and horses led by James II's son Berwick. William, on the opposite side of the Boyne, was viewing the clash through a field glass with a degree of anguish. His Secretary at War, George Clarke, recorded: 'The King was in a good deal of apprehension for them, there not being any hedge or ditch before them nor any of our horse to support them, and I was so near His Majesty as to hear him say softly to himself, "my poor guards, my poor guards, my poor guards".'

'there are your persecutors!'

James Fitzjames, Duke of Berwick, Earl of Tynemouth and Baron Bosworth, illegitimate son of James II and Arabella Churchill, had, at the age of nineteen, gathered a considerable reputation as a soldier. In many ways he was like his cousin John Churchill, the Earl of Marlborough (soon to be raised to a dukedom) who was twenty years his senior. Berwick had already seen some hard campaigns during his service with the Duke of Lorraine's army against the Turks and in Hungary under Lieutenant-General Taafe, whose brother Francis, the third earl of Carlingford now served in his command. In fifty-two days' time, God willing, Berwick would celebrate his twentieth birthday as the youngest cavalry general of his day. By his side, as Berwick ordered his horse into line for the charge against the seemingly imperturbable Dutch Guards, was his seventeen-year-old brother Henry, Grand Prior of England, who had preferred to stay with his brother than to follow his regiment towards Rosnaree. The Fitzjames brothers had been sent to France to be educated as Catholics. They had studied at La Flèche under the Jesuits, and were ardent for their father's cause.

The first Jacobite charge broke against the Dutch like water against a stone breakwater. Now that pikes were being given up, the main weapon for repulsing cavalry by infantry was the *chevaux-de-frise*, an arrangement of spikes formed from bayonets held on muskets. The Dutch were one of the few Williamite regiments so equipped. The toll among the Jacobites was heavy and Lord Carlingford was among the first of those killed. The Dutch still stood impenetrable in their squares as the Jacobite horse wheeled away.

Lieutenant-General Dominic Sheldon urged his mount forward and rallied them into a second charge. Again the Jacobite cavalry formed up and hurled itself against the Dutch. Again they were beaten off with considerable losses, Sheldon having his horse killed under him and Colonel Sutherland receiving a severe wound. William, observing the valiant efforts of his Dutch troops, was delighted. George Clarke reported that 'when he saw them stand their ground and fire by platoons, so that the horse were forced to run away in great disorder, he breathed out as people used to after holding their breath upon a fright or suspense, and said he had seen his Guards do that which he had never seen foot do in his life'. The Danish ambassador was standing near William, also observing the attack, and he said of the Dutch regiment: 'It defended itself so bravely that the Irish were twice obliged to retire with heavy loss and the Dutch remained masters of the position.'

The Duke of Schomberg, for all his eighty-four years, was riding about the field, trying to detect every weakness and rally the men. But he was worried. The colonial regiments had not yet crossed the river to support the Dutch and neither had the division of Huguenots and English. The Danish ambassador recalled:

> The Duke of Schomberg, who had not yet crossed the river . . . seeing that if King James' bodyguard returned to the charge, the Dutch regiment might be overwhelmed, hastened to bring it assistance by urging the regiments mentioned, together with some cavalry squadrons, to cross with all speed. To ensure the success of the manoeuvre he himself crossed. Scarcely had he reached the opposite bank when King James' bodyguard returned to the charge for the third time and with such intrepidity that it at length succeeded in breaking the lines of the Dutch Regiment, which had not yet got support from the troops despatched for the purpose. They were, however, already in the river, and were firing from a distance on the Irish, who urged on by too great a zeal had rashly ventured as far as the streets of the village. This gave us an opportunity of cutting them off, so that very few remained and our troops were left masters of the situation.

It was now about eleven o'clock and, with the Duke of Schomberg on the other side of the river, William decided to establish another bridgehead further downstream. He decided to throw across the Danish division under the German Lieutenant-General Ferdinand Wilhelm, Duke of Würtemburg-Neustadt. They would cross over the extreme east of Yellow Island, about a mile from Oldbridge, forming up for a flanking attack. The Danish foot and cavalry would be reinforced by Colonel John Cutts' Dutch infantry and La Mellionière's French division, consisting of five foot battalions and six squadrons of horse. The writer of the anonymous Danish Journal observed that the division was ordered to the attack by Würtemburg-Neustadt. 'Orders were therefore given that everyone should be ready to march and that the musketeers should strike their tents and leave their greatcoats and knapsacks with the tents.'

Not yet knowing of the failure of Sheldon's cavalry to dislodge the Dutch, Richard Hamilton had led his body of foot against the Huguenot regiments of Caillimote and Cambron while the Earl of Antrim's foot, on his left flank, pitted themselves against Count Nassau's regiment. Hamilton's infantry were a collection of raw recruits, those who had enlisted that spring, poorly trained and even more poorly armed. As Hamilton led them down the river bank and they saw the regiments of Nassau and Hanmer with those of Caillimote and Cambron wading across the river, they broke and fled, leaving Hamilton in midstream waving his sword and pleading with them to remain and fight. Seeing that it was a hopeless task, and realising, as musket balls whistled dangerously past his head, how perilous his position was, Hamilton spurred his horse up the bank after his fleeing soldiers. He suddenly came upon a squadron of cavalry looking lost and waiting for direction. Waving his sword towards the Boyne, Hamilton rallied them into a battle line and charged at their head back to the river bank where Hanmer and Nassau had managed to wade ashore.

Lord Antrim's regiment had become entangled with the fleeing soldiers of Hamilton's foot and they, too, had panicked. The four Williamite regiments were securing themselves on the south bank as Hamilton returned to the attack with his squadron of cavalry. As the Jacobite horse smashed into Nassau and Hanmer's troops some twenty of the cavalrymen fell from their horses under a withering musket fire but the rest, carried on by the momentum of their charge, swept along the river bank and even through the regiments of Caillimote and Cambron.

Gustavus Hamilton's Enniskillen regiment of foot, with Colonel Wolseley's Enniskillen horse, had now joined forces with the Dutch Guards at Oldbridge and the east flank of these regiments, seeing the remnants of Richard Hamilton's cavalry squadron ploughing through the Huguenot troops, set up a volley fire as the cavalrymen swept into them. Of the original sixty soldiers of the squadron, only six to eight survived with Hamilton, miraculously unscathed, at their head. No sooner had Hamilton reached the main body of Jacobite horse again than he demanded from a rueful Sheldon, who had just had his second horse killed under him, another squadron of cavalry. This squadron he led in another attack against Nassau and Hanmer and so fiercely did he press them that they were driven back into the river. Story mistakenly thought that the Jacobite cavalry was commanded by Berwick and not Hamilton. For a while the two sides faced each other, exchanging musket and pistol fire. According to Story, after a while 'Berwick's' men began to advance.

> . . . and as they advanced one that had been formerly in Sir John Hanmer's regiment came out singly and called one of the captains by name, who stepping towards him, the other fired his pistols at him, but was taken prisoner; this troop was beat off again with the loss of only three of Sir John Hanmer's men.

The fighting here lasted nearly half an hour. Story says: 'Much about this time there was nothing to be seen but smoke and dust nor anything to be heard but one continued fire for nigh half an hour . . .' Caillimote's regiment suffered heavy casualties in this exchange with Colonel La Caillimote himself receiving a mortal wound. He was carried back across the river crying '*à la gloire, mes enfants, à la gloire!*' But the thoughts of the shattered men of his regiment were far from ideas of glory. Badly broken, they threatened to run. It was then that the aged Duke of Schomberg and his staff raced up. The Duke, assessing the situation, pulled out his sword and waved it at the advancing Jacobite cavalry.

'*Allons, messieurs, voilà vos persecuteurs!*'

'Come, gentlemen, there are your persecutors!' he cried, appealing to the emotions of the Huguenot soldiers. The appeal had the desired effect for the regiment rallied.

The Jacobite cavalry, now reinforced by Tyrconnell's regiment, with Tyrconnell leading them himself, were charging the Williamites yet again. This time they were reinforced by Lord Galmoy's eight troops of fifty horse, who had been on the road towards Rosnaree when they heard of the Oldbridge attack and turned back. They were led by thirty-eight-year-old Pierce Butler, the third Viscount Galmoy, a cousin to the Williamite James Butler, Duke of Ormonde. Thus reinforced, the Jacobite cavalry made their finest charge yet.

The commander of the Danish division, Würtemburg-Neustadt, states that it was eleven o'clock when he started to move across the river by Yellow Island. He decided to move his infantry across first to establish a bridgehead, leaving his three cavalry regiments under the command of his Major-General of Horse, Frédéric Henri, Marquis de la Forest-Suzannet, a

Huguenot nobleman who had once been Danish envoy to London. With his Major-General of Foot, the East Prussian Julius Ernst von Tettau, who had directed much of the engineering work on the campaign, and his divisional Adjutant-General Hans Georg Walter, Würtemburg-Neustadt directed the eight foot regiments across the river personally, spearheaded by his own Guard's regiment. The Danes were a well-armed force, each soldier having the latest flintlock musket with bayonet. By means of their bayonets the Danes were able to counter many of the Jacobite cavalry charges with the defensive *chevaux-de-frise* while, as Würtemburg-Neustadt pointed out, it was the lack of such protection that overwhelmed the regiments of Cambron and Caillimote. Each Danish regiment's fittest men were made into grenadier companies and, armed with swords and hand grenades, they acted as shock troops. The infantry officers and non-commissioned officers carried espontons or half pikes, or halberds. The cavalry regiments were armed with long swords and protected by breast and back plates.

Writing to Christian V of Denmark five days later, Würtemburg-Neustadt recalled: 'Where your Majesty's Guards crossed, the water was so deep that it came up to their armpits. We marched across by division. The bottom was very boggy.' The anonymous author of the Danish Journal observed: 'As, however, the water was so deep that in places it came up to the belts, and in other places, to the armpits, progress was slow and difficult. Meanwhile the enemy began to advance on the left flank and fired a heavy salvo.'

Würtemburg-Neustadt 'was himself the first of the Guards to enter and cross the water'. According to de la Fouleresse, Würtemburg-Neustadt was carried across the river by the tallest of his grenadiers. The Jacobites advancing on the left flank of the Danes were Berwick and Galmoy, backed by Oliver O'Gara's infantry regiment. Seeing their approach the Danes began to hurry across in order that they should not be caught in midstream. In their hurry many of them missed the line of the ford and found themselves up to their necks in the water while trying to hold their muskets and powder high above their heads. But the Danes managed to reach the south bank before the Jacobites could close. Würtemburg-Neustadt remembered that 'while we were marching out of the water a squadron of dragoons came up and attacked the Guards. I allowed only the

grenadiers and some platoons to charge on which the enemy
was repulsed.' But it was not as simple as that because as the
Danes were trying to form up to protect their bridgehead 'they
were vigorously attacked' by a troop of Irish horse. Story says:
'They charged the Danes so home that they came faster back
again than then went, some of them never looking behind till
they had crossed the river again.' But Würtemberg-Neustadt,
by means of good bayonet work, established his bridgehead.
The Danish account states that 'the enemy horse advanced on
our Guards but they found the chevaux de frise and vigorous
firing and they retired again'. Würtemburg-Neustadt explained
that 'the enemy forces would not attack again with their cavalry,
giving the excuse, according to prisoners' statements, that they
were afraid of the chevaux de frise'. The fighting had been
tough for a while and according to one observer, Andreas
Claudinus, Würtemburg-Neustadt is said to have been captured
by an Irish soldier who thought he had captured William himself. The Irishman was determined to take Würtemburg-
Neustadt alive but the commander of the Danish troops is said
to have fended him off till a Danish captain came up from
behind and plunged his sword up to the hilt in the Irishman's
bowels. If Claudinus' story is true it is odd that no one else
mentioned the adventure.

As soon as the Danish Guard's bridgehead was secured the
main body of the Danish infantry began to cross. Then came
the cavalry regiments and these were supported by La
Mellionière's French and Cutts' Dutch troops.

The fighting from the Jacobite point of view was now desperate. The Williamites were pouring across the Boyne in a never-
ending tide and still they had plenty of men in reserve, for they
had not committed their dragoons or the bulk of their cavalry.
Tyrconnell tried to stem the onrushing tide with a ferocious
charge in which he decided to commit all his cavalry.

The charging one thousand men swept down the slopes of
Donore and burst against the Williamite positions from Oldbridge along the river bank to the east of Yellow Island.
Against such superior numbers the charge was a futile gesture
and the Jacobites paid dearly. But even the Williamites had to
admit their admiration. Lieutenant-General Douglas commented: 'The enemy's horse fought wonderfully bravely as ever men
could do.' Bellingham wrote that 'the enemy advanced towards

us and made brisk effort upon us. The enemy's horse of Tyrconnell's regiment behaved themselves well but our Dutch like
angels.' More sardonically Würtemburg-Neustadt said 'they
fought so well that their infantry gained enough time to save
themselves'. The Jacobite regiment which suffered most from
the charge was the cavalry of John Parker. Parker's family had
been settled in Ireland for many years and an ancestor had been
constable of Dublin Castle in 1543. His father William had
started his career as an excise officer and then decided to become
a physician, opening a practice in Margate. In 1664 he had
been made an Honorary Fellow of the College of Physicians.
His son John, however, born in 1654, decided on a military
career, securing a commission as captain in the Duke of York's
regiment. By 1687 he was lieutenant-colonel in the same regiment and the next year he followed James to France and then
on to Ireland. Of the four hundred men of Parker's regiment
that took part in that courageous charge against the Williamites
only thirty men survived unscathed. Parker himself received a
serious wound and his lieutenant-colonel and major were killed.

During the charge Berwick had his horse killed under him.
His father later wrote that 'the Duke of Berwick, having his
horse shot under him, was some time amongst the enemy, he
was rode over and ill bruised, however, by the help of a trooper,
got off again'.

The charge that killed many Jacobites, however, also killed
the Captain-General of the Williamite army, the old Duke of
Schomberg. There were, in fact, many casualties among the
Williamites where the defensive bayonet and pikes were lacking.
As the Williamite cavalry had not yet been committed at Oldbridge there was no way to counter-attack in order to drive back
the Jacobite horse. Story says 'the want of horse was so apparent
at this place'. He goes further in an effort—a rather far-fetched
one—to link this with the inactivity of Count Schomberg's
division facing James' main force across the bog. At Oldbridge,
he says, 'people cried out Horse! Horse! which word going
towards the right and they mistaking it for Halt! stopped the
right wing nigh half an hour; which time spent might have done
service'.

Therefore, as the charge swept down on Oldbridge, at just
about noon that day, it swept up to where the Duke of Schomberg was directing the Huguenot and Enniskillen regiments. He

received three sabre cuts over the head and one in the face but it was a musket ball striking him in the neck that tumbled him from his horse. The Danish ambassador wrote to his King that Schomberg 'was struck in the neck by the bullet of a carbine, as it is presumed, by our own men, who were crossing the river and discharging their pieces as they advanced. The shot threw the Duke from his horse. He fell on a very stony path and this doubtless contributed to hasten the great man's death.' Williamite rumour had it that the bullet was fired inadvertently by a trooper of Cambron's regiment. The Jacobite claim was that Sir Cathal O'Toole of the Royal Regiment of Foot had recognised Schomberg and shot him just before he was killed himself. A Captain Foubert who was next to Schomberg, and had also been wounded in his arm, dismounted to help the Duke but, says the Williamite doctor, Mullenaux, 'he died immediately without uttering a word'.

The same charge also killed George Walker, the bishop-designate of Derry, who had been acting as chaplain to the Enniskillen regiments. According to George Story he had gone to Schomberg's assistance when he was struck down. This was not very likely and it was more plausible that he was merely fighting with Hamilton's Enniskillen Foot. He received a wound in the stomach which he survived only a few minutes. Story says his body was 'stripped immediately for the Scotch-Irish that followed our camp were got through already and took off most of the plunder'.

It was reported that when the news of Walker's death was brought to William, who disliked militaristic priests, he asked sarcastically: 'What took him there?' George Walker had come under attack from many quarters as a man of God who had taken up arms. He had answered his critics in his *Vindication of the True Account of the Siege of Londonderry*.

His case has all the authority that the greatest necessity in the world can give to any action, he wrote. The lives of thousands beside his own were at stake, his religion, that is dearer than all, and the English and Scots (equally dear to him) next door to an utter extirpation out of Ireland, not to speak of the dangers of others, how can anyone imagine that there should be an obligation upon any man that can exempt or excuse his unconcernedness in such a case?

Walker's body was buried where it had fallen by a volunteer from Donaghmore, Co. Meath. Some time later Walker's

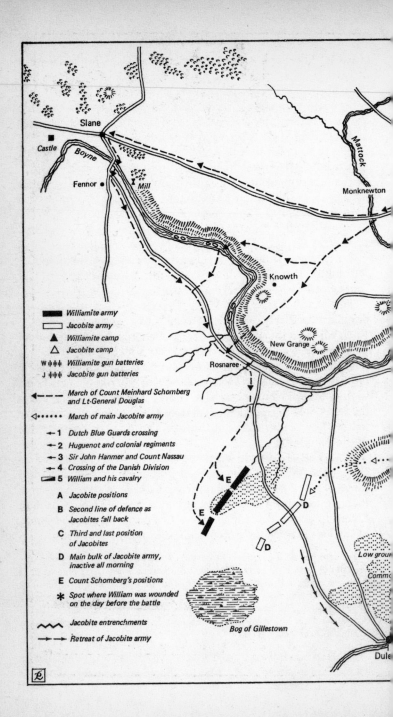

▰	**Williamite army**
▢	**Jacobite army**
▲	**Williamite camp**
△	**Jacobite camp**
W ⫼⫼	**Williamite gun batteries**
J ⫼⫼	**Jacobite gun batteries**

◄------- **March of Count Meinhard Schomberg and Lt-General Douglas**

◁•••••• **March of main Jacobite army**

←─1 *Dutch Blue Guards crossing*

←─2 *Huguenot and colonial regiments*

←─3 *Sir John Hanmer and Count Nassau*

←─4 *Crossing of the Danish Division*

▰─5 *William and his cavalry*

A *Jacobite positions*

B *Second line of defence as Jacobites fall back*

C *Third and last position of Jacobites*

D *Main bulk of Jacobite army, inactive all morning*

E *Count Schomberg's positions*

✳ *Spot where William was wounded on the day before the battle*

〰〰 *Jacobite entrenchments*

→──► *Retreat of Jacobite army*

Slane
Castle
Boyne
Fennor •
Mill
Mattock
Monknewton
Knowth
New Grange
Rosnaree
E
E
D
D
Low grou
Comm
Bog of Gillestown
Dule

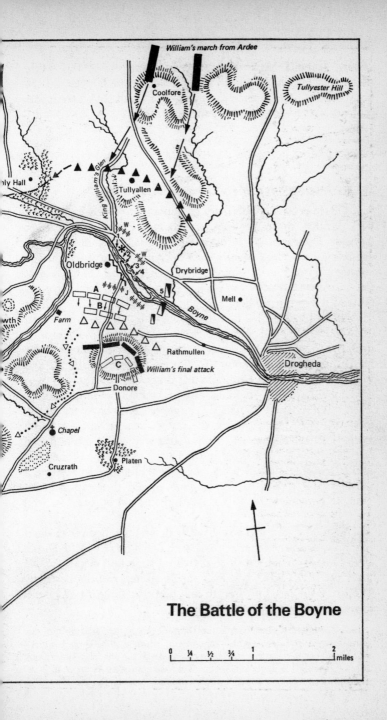

William's march from Ardee

Coolfore

Tullyester Hill

King William's Glen

Tullyallen

nly Hall

W

Oldbridge

W

Drybridge

A

J

Mell

Farm

Boyne

wth

Rathmullen

C

William's final attack

Donore

Chapel

Cruzrath

Platen

Drogheda

The Battle of the Boyne

0   ¼   ½   ¾   1   2 miles

widow, Isabella Maxwell, returned to the site of the battle with a servant who had been with Walker at the Boyne, and the body was disinterred and taken to Castle Caulfield where it was reburied on the south side of the chancel in 1702.

'are you angry with your friends?'

Just before receiving the news of Schomberg's death, William had decided to make another crossing further down river towards Drogheda with dragoons and cavalry in order to encircle the Jacobite cavalry now delaying his advance. As the commander of this division he chose Godart de Ginkel, eldest son of Godart Adriann van Reede, Baron Ginkel, from Utrecht. Ginkel, a veteran soldier, had gone to England with William in 1688 and had gained a reputation by his ruthless suppression of a mutiny in a Scottish regiment at Harwick when they declared themselves for James. William ordered Ginkel to take his Dutch cavalry regiment of 152 men, together with the 258 soldiers of Sir Albert Cuningham's dragoons and the 246 men of Colonel Levison's dragoons, and find a ford further upstream. Tyrconnell noticed Ginkel's regiments commence to march along the river bank towards the east and immediately ordered Lord Walter Dongan, whose dragoons were still fresh and had not, as yet, been committed in the battle, to ride along the crest of the hills of Rathmullen, keeping the Williamites in sight on a parallel course, and to harass them should they try to cross. Dongan's regiment, at full strength, consisted of four hundred men.

The midday sun was now beating down fiercely on the sweating, powder-stained men. It had been two hours since the Dutch Blue Guards struck up their marching tune and began to ford the river into Oldbridge. Still the Jacobites, outnumbered by William's soldiers by three to one, were holding up William's crossing.

It was about this time, [wrote the Danish ambassador] that an aide-de-camp brought the news of his [Schomberg] death to the King. I noticed that he did not say a word. He only made a sign to the officer to say nothing about it, laying his finger on his lip. This was doubtless in order that the troops, who were very fond of him, should not be alarmed at the news. This sad intelligence, which afflicted the King more than he wished to show, hastened his crossing over to the other side of the river, so as to maintain the troops in the good order in which we saw them fighting. He went over about a quarter of an hour later.

The aide was Schomberg's equerry (écuyer) Monsieur de Montorqis. According to George Clarke, standing close to William with M. de la Fouleresse, 'the King had immediate notice of it [Schomberg's death] by one of the Duke's aides-de-camp but did not seem much concerned'. Clarke, of course, was already prejudiced about William's coldness to Schomberg but, on the other hand, it was probably true that William was not exactly disheartened by the death of the man upon whom he had blamed the military failures in Ireland. What was certain, however, was that Schomberg's death could have a very adverse effect on the morale of the army and therefore William decided that it was high time he crossed the river himself and took a part in the battle. He decided to follow Ginkel and take the main body of his trusty Dutch cavalry and the regiments of the Dutch Horse Guards, a total of 1,500 fresh troops.

The ford that Ginkel had chosen was a bad one. The river was deep here and made even deeper by the displacement of water by the Williamite troops already struggling across by Oldbridge, Grove Island and Yellow Island. Bentinck said that the 'horses were fain to swim'. The ford was about a mile and a half from Oldbridge, where the little stream of Drybridge emptied itself into the Boyne from the north and where a smaller riverlet also met the Boyne on the south bank. On this south bank the ground rose rapidly to a height of one hundred feet within a few yards. Dumont de Bostaquet, a Huguenot cavalry-man, claims that his regiment was the first to cross the river after the news of Schomberg's death for, just before they began to cross, they heard the news of 'Schomberg's death, of there having been fierce fighting and of many of our officers having been killed and wounded'. It would appear from this that de Bostaquet was serving in Ginkel's Dutch cavalry and this is confirmed by the geography of the ford he crossed by because he relates how he had to swim across with his horse.

William caught up with Ginkel as the crossing was being made. On the opposite bank the Williamites could see Lord Walter Dongan's dragoons leaving the hills of Rathmullen to get nearer the water's edge to prevent the crossing. William himself ordered up two field guns to give Ginkel covering fire. Some Danish foot soldiers were ordered to this crossing and told to give volley fire coverage to the Dutch cavalry. Lord Dongan was killed by one of the first cannon shots and several of his men were mowed down, killed or wounded. The fire from the two field guns and the withering musket fire broke the rest of his regiment and they took to their heels, galloping off across the hills in the direction of Duleek. Some braver members of the regiment managed to retrieve the body of their colonel and eventually to carry it to Castletown, in Co. Limerick, where they gave the son of the Earl of Limerick a soldier's burial.

With the opposition scattered William started to cross himself. He was still clad in his decorations, bearing the colourful Star and Garter, and was a prominent target for any enterprising Jacobite sniper. Lieutenant-General Douglas, now on the right wing with Count Schomberg, said that William's wound had caused such stiffness that William could hardly carry a sword. Bentinck, riding with the King, says that William carried his sword in his left hand. The Danish ambassador claimed that William carried nothing but a walking stick, but he had removed himself to a respectful distance from the King's party. As he wrote to Christian V: 'Mr Hoy and I followed him at a distance, not deeming it our duty to expose ourselves to musket shot and sabre cuts.'

William had trouble in crossing. His horse became bogged down and he had to dismount and have the animal dragged out of the mud. Tradition has it that an Enniskillener named Mackinlay performed this service although the Enniskillen regiments were nowhere near this area. Sir Robert Southwell, writing to the Earl of Nottingham, says the crossing was so boggy that the King 'was fain to walk three or four hundred paces so as to be near out of breath'. In spite of this asthmatic attack, William soon remounted and was leading a total of near two thousand cavalry in an encircling movement towards Oldbridge.

The remnants of Lord Dongan's dragoons had halted and joined forces with the dragoon regiment of Viscount Clare. Clare's regiment, in their distinctive yellow uniforms, which earned them the title of the 'Yellow Dragoons', was the only regiment that stood between William and the unguarded right flank of the Jacobites. Clare lined up his dragoons and charged the Williamite horse as if they were cavalry. Dumont de Bostaquet says that the Irish charged like madmen and that his regiment, presumably Ginkel's Dutchmen, were driven back. Story is not so charitable about Clare's bravery for he sneeringly claims that the Irish horsemen 'that charged so desperately were drunk with brandy, each man that morning having received half a pint to his share; but it seems the foot had not so large a portion, or at least they did not deserve it so well'. Brandy had, indeed, been issued to the troops that morning for it was a standard military practice in every army, though it was said that the Jacobites had made a rush for the barrels and helped themselves more liberally than was intended. The Jacobite Stevens, trying to apportion the blame, said that the brandy ration had been supplied too liberally. 'I am sure above 1,000 men were thereby rendered unfit for service and many were left dead drunk scattered about the fields.' Had this been true, however, Williamite propaganda would not have been slow to mention the fact. Stevens, of course, knew little of what was happening at Oldbridge. Indeed, he seems to have unjustly slighted Clare's dragoons, saying that Clare had behaved 'shamefully!' He goes on: 'There is no place of excuse for the dragoons, especially the Earl [sic] of Clare's, commonly known by the name yellow dragoons being the colour of their colours, who were the first that fled having scarce seen the enemy.' It was true that after the initial success with their first charge against Ginkel's cavalry, Clare's dragoons were forced to fall back but in fairly good order. This left one Jacobite foot regiment, Oliver O'Gara's regiment, facing the oncoming Williamite horse.

A family drama was played out at this point. In O'Gara's regiment was one William Mulloy and his seventeen-year-old nephew, Charles Mulloy. Opposing them, as a Captain of Williamite dragoons, was William's brother Theobold, the father of Charles. Tradition has it that Theobold presented his horse to William when William's horse was shot. However, in the ensuing conflict young Charles Mulloy was captured by the dragoons of his father's regiment but because of Charles' age and his father's service for William the boy was pardoned and sent home.

With the Williamite cavalry across the Boyne in strength, there seemed little hope for Jacobite resistance. The weight of

their numbers caused the Jacobite infantry to begin to panic.
James wrote:

> But at the same time the enemy's horse began to cross the river which the
> King's Foot perceiving immediately gave way, notwithstanding, all that
> Dorrington and the officers could do to stop them which cost several of the
> captains their lives as Arundel, Ashton, Dongan, Fitzgerald and two or
> three more, besides the Marquis de Hoquincourt who was killed with
> several of his brigade.

Berwick recalled:

> . . . but their cavalry, having found means to pass at another ford, and
> advancing to fall upon our foot, I brought up our horse, which gave our
> battalions an opportunity to retreat; but at the same time we had a very
> unequal combat to sustain, as well from the number of squadrons, as from
> the badness of the ground, which was cut through in many places, and into
> which the enemy had introduced infantry.

As the Jacobite foot fell back, causing the infantry all along
the line from Drybridge to Oldbridge to follow suit, many of
them throwing aside their muskets and taking to their heels, all
that remained between William's troops and the flying men
were the cavalry regiments of Tyrconnell, Sutherland and the
thirty survivors from Parker's decimated regiment, Berwick's
two troops of depleted Horse Guards, and the remnants of
Dongan and Clare's dragoons. All accounted for, a total of little
under 1,000 men, weary after two to three hours of continuous
battle, faced a victorious army of 15,000 troops, many of whom
had not yet even lifted their muskets. The Jacobite horse were
not wanting and Berwick says they 'charged and charged again
ten times, until the enemy, amazed at our boldness, halted'.

Ginkel's regiment, having recovered and reformed, was led in
a charge along a little lane which led to Oldbridge, close along
the river bank from Drogheda. His charge was met by a head-
first counter charge led by the indomitable Dominic Sheldon
who turned Ginkel back. Ginkel, who was 'much vexed in
retreating', halted several hundred yards down the lane as the
Jacobite cavalry was brought to a standstill by Sheldon. A
Captain Brewerton, in command of two companies of Levison's
dragoons, was acting as flanking cover to Ginkel on each side
of the lane. He had seen the Jacobites charge past in pursuit of
Ginkel, and unaware of his two troops behind the hedges that
bordered the lane. He ordered his men to dismount and take
up ambush positions, ready to fire at the Jacobites when they

returned from their charge. Ginkel had, in the meantime, re-organised his Dutchmen and charged the halted Jacobite cavalry as they were returning back down the lane. Sheldon had no time to turn his horse to meet the charge so he urged them forward, back in the direction of Oldbridge. Ginkel, in close pursuit, 'was in some danger by our own dragoons', wrote Dumont de Bostaquet, 'for the enemy being close upon him, they could not well distinguish, however, the dragoons did here a piece of good service in stopping the enemy, who came up very boldly and our horse rallying both here and to the right, after near half an hour's dispute, the enemy were again beaten from this place'.

The Jacobite horse now withdrew, in good order, to the slopes of Donore. The Williamites were consolidated on the south side of the Boyne and Percy Kirk had taken over at Old-bridge with Henry Sidney, the colonel of William's English Foot Guards, as his second-in-command. They 'went from one place to another as the posture of affairs required their prefer-ence'. William began to close in on Donore from the east. It was at this point that Tyrconnell realised the hopelessness of the situation and decided to try to make an orderly retreat to Duleek. He ordered Richard Hamilton to take command of the rearguard and delay the Williamites as best he could, then left the field with Major-General Dorrington in the wake of the fleeing infantry. Hamilton, pressing back on Donore, made a courageous defence, holding the Jacobite horse tightly to-gether.

William racing forward, seeing victory in his grasp, rode up to the nearest cavalry regiment—the Enniskilleners, com-manded by the tough and forceful Englishman, Colonel William Wolseley, who had been responsible for the striking Williamite victory on July 30, 1689, at Newtownbutler, when he had defeated a force twice his strength. The success, Wolseley had modestly said, was due to the excellence of his officers and marksmanship of his men. Newtownbutler had given the Enniskilleners their reputation and encouraged William to use them prominently in the battle. Now he called to the 423 men of the regiment: 'What will you do for me?' In the dust and smoke no one recognised him and several troopers levelled their pistols at his person. Then Wolseley spied the Star and Garter and cried: 'It's the King!' The Enniskilleners raised a cheer. William, standing up in his stirrups, cried: 'Gentlemen, you shall be my guards today. I have heard much of you. Let me see something of you!'

He then led them up the hill under a tremendous Jacobite fire. A broadsheet entitled *An account of King William's royal heading of the men of Inniskillin*, published some weeks later in London, recounted that William had told the Enniskilleners 'that he had heard a great character of them, and therefore would do them the honour to head them himself, which accordingly he performed; for after they had passed the ford he charged at the head of them and they fought like tigers'. William led them up to the old ruined church at the top of the hill of Donore where Hamilton's men had dismounted and dug in. In the heat, dust and smoke, it was almost impossible to tell friend from foe. But William seemed to lead a charmed life. He was struck by two Jacobite musket balls, one of which grazed the cap of his pistol and the other carried off the heel of his boot.

Southwell says that Hamilton had lined the walls of the churchyard with musketeers. The Enniskilleners made their assault on the north side of the walls at the same time as some Dutch troops made an assault on the south side.

[They] did very bravely at first, [wrote Southwell] but espying another great party, whom they took for the enemy, just ready to surround them, they began to fly and did actively put in disorder the Dutch horse and all others that stood in their way. The place was unfortunately full of holes and dung pits and the passages narrow; but above all the dust and smoke quite blinded them. His Majesty was here in the crowd of all, drawing his sword and animating them that fled to follow him. His danger was great among the enemy's guns which killed thirty of the Inniskilliners on the spot. Nay one of the Inniskilliners came with a pistol cocked to His Majesty, till he called out 'what, are you angry with your friends?' The truth is, the clothes of friends and foes are so much alike that His Majesty had had goodness to excuse all that passed.

The Jacobites put up a very fierce resistance on Donore. The Duke of Würtemberg-Neustadt recalled:

When we crossed and were mounting the hill, we found the enemy dragoons and troopers more inclined to fight than the infantry, which hurried away before us so fast that our men could never engage them. The enemy horse advanced on our Guards but as they found there the chevaux de frise and vigorous firing they retired again.

Hamilton realised that if he remained on Donore it would not be long before the Williamites would completely cut him off and overrun the position. And once the high ground at Donore was taken, the Oldbridge sector would become untenable for the Jacobites. This would pose an immediate threat to the Jacobite left which could well be hemmed in between the two prongs of William's army. William seemed to realise this as well for he had rejoined his Dutch Guards and was concentrating the whole of his attack on the hilltop. Hamilton drew his cavalry back down the road to Platen Castle. This road ran straight south to Platen and then swung westward to join the main Oldbridge to Duleek roadway. The Williamites pressed closely after him so that before he reached Platen he had to draw up his cavalry once again and charge them. Hamilton routed the Enniskilleners with considerable losses so that they broke their formation and fell back into the Danish cavalry of Montz Melchoir von Donop. In the confusion von Donop mistook the colonists for Jacobite cavalry who, in turn, thought von Donop's men were a Jacobite force. According to the Danish Journal, 'when the Inniskilliners on one occasion pressed the enemy too close, he chased them back on our cavalry. I certainly believe that in the confusion and the thick dust they and Donop's regiment charged one another in the belief they were charging the enemy'. But it was so easy to mistake friend and foe. Many of the soldiers in the conflict had lost their white pieces of paper, which passed for white cockades, or their sprigs of green. The Huguenot trooper, Dumont de Bostaquet, recalled that he was about to run through a man he took to be a Jacobite when the man called out 'I'm an Enniskillener' and de Bostaquet suddenly realised the man was wearing a sprig of green in his hat.

In that last charge of the Jacobite cavalry, Lieutenant-General Richard Hamilton had been wounded and taken prisoner. According to de la Fouleresse, Hamilton was captured within a few paces of William and his captors had rushed to kill him when the King saw who it was and cried out to them not to do so. William rode over and peered down at the wounded man and, with a wry humour, said he was glad to see him. Would, he asked, the Jacobite cavalry charge his troops again? Hamilton nodded. 'Yes, upon my honour, I believe they will for they have a good body of horse still.'

William raised an eyebrow disdainfully. 'Your honour?' he asked slowly, emphasising the first word.

The Danish ambassador explained to Christian V that 'this is the same who, having faithlessly accepted the mission entrusted to him by the King of coming over to this country for the purpose of persuading Tyrconnell to submit, instead of using his influence, which he possessed over the latter, to induce him to take this step, encouraged him in supporting the interests of King James'. When Hamilton had joined Tyrconnell and the Jacobites in 1689 a Williamite observer commented: 'The Papists lit bonfires when Dick Hamilton came over; they said he was worth ten thousand men.' He had certainly proved that at the Boyne. Hamilton's brothers, Anthony and John, with James' main body, believed that their brother had been killed at the Boyne but a few days later a French officer told them that he had been seen as a prisoner riding to Dublin. William had ordered his own surgeon to dress Hamilton's wounds on the field and some days later he was taken to the Tower of London. He was eventually exchanged for the Williamite William Stewart, first Viscount Mountjoy, who had been imprisoned in the Bastille the previous year.

With the loss of Hamilton, the Duke of Berwick took command of the Jacobite cavalry. He regrouped them again and led them in good order slowly past Platen, swinging westward to gain the main road to Duleek. According to Story, 'Colonel Levison, with a part of his dragoons, got between some of the enemy horse and Duleek and killed several, yet if they had not minded retreating more than fighting he might have come off a loser'. But it would have been fatal for the Jacobite cavalry, now numbering far less than its initial thousand troopers, to stand and fight and allow the main body of Williamite troops to come up and surround them. Uppermost in the young Duke of Berwick's mind was how to get his small cavalry detachment to safety across the River Nanny at Duleek.

'sheep flying before the wolf'

It was just after two o'clock when the red-faced aide-de-camp galloped up to King James and told him that 'the enemy had forced the pass at Oldbridge and that the right was beaten'. James realised that he had committed a gross error by moving two-thirds of his army to the left, to an area where the Williamites had only made a feint, leaving Oldbridge too weakly protected. There was only one way to reduce the balance. James, for all that was said about him afterwards, tried to do so. He 'whispered to M de Lauzun that there was no time to be lost, that the attack must be made before the troops were informed of what had passed on the right, which was the only chance of recovering the affair'.

The Marquis de la Hoguette, Lauzun's Maréchal de Camp, was ordered to take command of the French troops to act as the vanguard of an attack on Count Schomberg's positions. The dragoon regiments of Robert Clifford, Francis Carroll and Thomas Maxwell were given orders to dismount and make ready their muskets. A wave of excitement broke over the men. Hours of inaction were about to be replaced with a battle at last. Just as the Jacobites were beginning to move, however, Partrick Sarsfield and Thomas Maxwell, who had been to reconnoitre the ground between the two armies, galloped up and reported to a frustrated James: 'It was impossible for the horse to charge the enemy by reason of two double ditches with high banks and a little brook between them that ran along the small valley that divided the two armies.'

James stood wavering in indecision. At that moment de la Hoguette galloped up and demanded to know of Lauzun why they were wasting time. Lauzun pointed out that the deep, narrow gorge and the bog prevented the Jacobite army from closing with the enemy. The cavalry commander, the Marquis Lery de Girardin, confirmed that it was impossible for the horse to charge the enemy across such terrain. De la Hoguette, writing to his superiors in France a few days later, says he answered that the bog was not so great and if there was a ravine it would be quite easy to cross it while the enemy were still at a distance. In any case, de la Hoguette claimed, seemingly anxious to show his own courage, the Jacobites were in such a position that they would have to beat the enemy or wait to be beaten.

But if there had been any way by which the Jacobites could have attacked the Williamites then Major-General Patrick Sarsfield would certainly have discovered it for Sarsfield, who was not to really show his talent as a formidable military commander until after the Boyne, was one of James' commanders who had long been advocating action. Sarsfield had been born at Lucan, near Dublin, in about 1650, the scion of an Old English family who had come to Ireland in 1172 as standard bearers to Henry II. His mother Anne was the daughter of Ruaraidh Ó Mordha, or Rory O'More, who had led the 1641 uprising and Sarsfield was fiercely Irish in sentiment. In September 1681 he had challenged Lord Grey to a duel for insulting the Irish. Sarsfield was educated at a French military college and then commissioned in the English army as a captain in Colonel Dongan's regiment of foot in 1678. By 1686 he had become a full colonel and assisted Tyrconnell in remodelling the Irish army. He had been in England at the time of William's landing and had followed James to France and then to Ireland, where he was given command of his own regiment and made a Privy Councillor. He had also served in the Irish Parliament, being returned for Co. Dublin. His service against the colonists in the north of Ireland had marked him out as a competent commander and one with courage and tenacity. He was fretful at being condemned to inactivity that morning and when he and Tom Maxwell went out to survey the terrain they were more than excited at the prospect of confronting the enemy. So de la Hoguette's implied criticism of Sarsfield, that the unsuitable ground was merely an excuse for not closing with Count Schomberg, cannot be taken seriously.

Suddenly the decision was taken out of the hands of the Jacobite generals. James records: 'At the same time the enemy's dragoons got on horseback and the whole line began to march by their flank to the right, and we soon lost sight of their van by a village that interposed; only by the dust that rose behind it they seemed to endeavour to gain the Dublin road.' If Count Schomberg and Lieutenant-General Douglas flanked the Jacobites and hemmed them in between themselves, the Boyne and William's victorious main army, then their position would become extremely awkward. Berwick wrote: 'In this situation the King, in order to avoid being hemmed in by that part of the enemy which had just forced the passage at Oldbridge, caused his troops to march by the left for the brook of Duleek.' Berwick was referring to the River Nanny.

Lauzun gave de la Hoguette orders to march off by the left flank towards Dublin. James was left for a moment looking enviously across the bog towards the dust left by the Williamite

troops marching southwards. As his army marched back on the
Rosnaree to Duleek road, James recalled:

> . . . the right wing's being beat was no longer a mystery for several of the
> scattered and wounded horsemen got in amongst them [his army] before
> they rode to Duleek; whereupon M. de Lauzun advised the King to take
> his own regiment of horse, which had the van of that wing, and some
> dragoons, and make the best of his way to Dublin for fear the enemy, who
> were so strong in horse and dragoon, should make detachments and get
> thither before him which he was confident they would endeavour to do, but
> that if His Majesty arrived there first he might, with the troops he had with
> him and the garrison he found there, prevent them possessing themselves of
> the town, that M. Lauzun could make the retreat which he prayed his leave
> to conduct.
>
> He then advised the King not to remain at Dublin, neither, but go with
> all expedition to France to prevent his falling into the enemy's hands which
> would be not only his but the prince, his son's, utter ruin, that as long as
> there was life there was hope and that if once he was in France again, his
> cause was not so desperate, they being in all probability masters at sea; that
> he would give one of his hands that he could have the honour to accompany
> him, but he must endeavour to make his retreat in the best manner possible
> he could or die with the French if they were beaten. This advice went much
> against the grain, so the King demur'd to it tho' reiterated several times but
> M. Lauzun ceased not pressing him till at last he found by a more particular
> account in what manner the business had been carried on the right, that all
> the enemy's army had passed the river which forced even the troops that
> were not beaten to retreat, and that by consequence it was necessary for him
> to do so too.

Lauzun began to panic a little and kept urging the cavalry
to go faster. De la Hoguette remonstrated with him and pointed
out that this would put the Jacobite infantry in danger but
Lauzun snapped back that nothing was to be thought of except
saving the person of King James. He ordered de la Hoguette not
to leave the King and detailed Sarsfield's regiment to act as an
escort. Both wings of the retreating Jacobite army were heading
on a collision course, for they were both making for the same
river crossing on the Nanny Water at the village of Duleek.
James later tried to justify his decision to take that line of retreat
by saying it was necessary because a bog higher up made the
Nanny impassable except at that point. However, the Jacobite
left could have retreated along the main road from Slane in
good order without colliding with the retreating men of Tyrconnell's division.

Captain Stevens recounted how the Grand Prior's regiment
was waiting for the order to engage with Count Schomberg's

men. They had already heard that Oldbridge 'was under attack
but the enemy had been repulsed by Lord Dongan who had
been killed'. The regiment was eager, 'vigorous and desirous of
battle', a thousand strong. To Stevens they looked invincible.
Then, came the surprising order to retire in the direction of
Duleek. The Grand Prior's regiment turned and began to march
down 'Duleek Lane' which, says Stevens, was a roadway 'enclosed in high banks'. The regiment was marching ten abreast
and in good order when a group of Jacobite horse, fleeing down
the lane, 'broke the whole line of foot, riding over all our
battalions'.

The horse came on so unexpected and with such speed, some firing their
pistols, that we had no time to receive or shun them, but all supposing them
to be the enemy (as indeed, they were no better to us) took to their heels, no
officer being able to stop the men ever after they were broken, and the horse
passed through, at the same time no enemy was near us or them that fled
in such haste to our destruction. . . . I wonder what madness possessed our
men to run so violently, nobody pursuing them?

Stevens tried to take command of the situation after the horse
had passed. 'What few men I could see I called to, no command
being of force, begging them to stand together and repair to
their colours, the danger being in dispersing, but all in vain,
some throwing away their arms, others even their coats and
shoes to run lighter.' Stevens climbed the banks of the roadway
to look round for the men. 'I thought the calamity had not been
so general till viewing the hills about us I perceived them
covered with soldiers of several regiments all scattered like
sheep flying before the wolf, but so thick they seemed to cover
the sides and tops of the hills.' He was horrified. 'The shame of
our regiment's dishonour only afflicted me before, but now all
the horror of a routed army, just before so vigorous and desirous
of battle, and broken without scarce a stroke from the enemy,
so perplexed my soul that I envied the few dead, and only
grieved I lived to be a spectator of so dismal and lamentable
a tragedy.'

Count Schomberg, now realising his enemy was retiring and
having the news from Oldbridge, began to pursue the Jacobites.
But Sir John Dalrymple, in a *Memoir*, says: 'The Count pursued but slowly; for he had no guide except the flying steps of
his enemy; and the bogs and ditches, which they who were
acquainted with their intricacies passed with ease, proved

obstacles to him every minute, so that whilst he thought he was gaining ground, he often found that he lost it.'

The Danish ambassador explained to Christian V that the pincer movement to encircle the entire Jacobite army did not materialise because of Count Schomberg's immobilisation in the bog. Instead of this immobilisation it would have been more effective for Schomberg and Douglas to move down the road from Slane towards Dublin and, according to James, this was what was happening when he gave the order to retire to Duleek. But, the Danish ambassador pointed out, Count Schomberg had no orders to cut off the enemy's retreat and William himself did not pursue the enemy as closely as he might have done, 'perhaps wishing to put into practice Caesar's maxim and leave his enemies a golden bridge' in order that they might escape.

He recalled that 'our cavalry, having formed itself into one body, some two miles beyond the camp of which we had taken possession [Oldbridge], pursued the enemy, but only slowly, till about nine or ten in the evening. Moreover, the small hills which surrounded the plain in which both armies had encamped favoured the enemy's flight.' But, he pointed out, the Williamite cavalry were 'exhausted with a twelve hour march'. Further, 'whilst the King was in pursuit of the enemy, both columns of our infantry were marching in good order, and just as though there had been no battle that day. Indeed, it may be said that this action was rather a rout than a battle. We know neither the loss of the enemy nor ours. It cannot be considerable on either side'.

The Jacobite Colonel O'Kelly claimed that it was the sight of the Jacobite army retreating in orderly fashion that caused William not to pursue them too closely. 'But the Prince of Orange, observing the King's army to make so good a countenance, thought it more prudent to halt, and suffer them to march away.' Bishop Burnet gave a more plausible reason which he had first hand from William himself. 'After James' army was broken up, William was of the opinion that the Irish would scatter and then surrender. A sharp pursuit would have accordingly brought about only a useless defeat. And he always had a horror of that.' In fact, Burnet amplified the subject of William's scruples on the defeat of James.

I had a particular occasion to know how tender he was of King James' person, having learned an instance of it from first hand; a proposition was

made to the King that a third rate ship, well manned by a faithful crew, and
commanded by one who had been well with King James, but was such a one
as the King (William) might trust, should sail to Dublin and declare for
King James. The person who told me this offered to be the man that should
carry the message to King James (for he was well known to him) to invite
him to come on board, which he seemed to be sure he would accept of, and
when he was aboard, they should sail away with him, and land him either
in Spain or Italy as the King desired; and should have £20,000 to give him
when he should be set ashore; the King thought it a well formed design and
likely enough to succeed but would not harken to it; he said he would have
no hand in treachery, and King James would certainly carry some of his
guards and of his court abroad with him and probably they would make
some opposition and in the struggle some accident might happen to the
King James' person, in which he would have no hand. I acquainted the
Queen with this and I saw in her a great tenderness for her father's person,
and she was much touched with the answer the King had made.

Bentinck was in favour of mounting a musketeer behind each
of 3,000 cavalry troopers to pursue the enemy but William
rejected the proposal. Story says that the Jacobites who did fall
into the hands of the Williamites were shown no mercy. 'Few
or none of the men escaped that came into their hands for they
shot them like hares amongst the corn and in the hedges as they
found them in their march.'

According to Stevens, the French regiments conducted 'a
most honourable retreat bringing off the cannon and marching
in very good order after sustaining the shock of the enemy'.
The French regiments, however, were never committed
throughout the action. Lauzun and de la Hoguette were later
criticised for cowardice and it was the colonel of the 'Blue'
regiment, Conrad von Zurlauben, whom Stevens praises. The
retreating troops from Oldbridge, having come off Cruzrath
Hill to the Nanny collided with the Jacobite troops from Rosnaree. There were several boggy fields with ditches just before
Duleek and in the midst of these a deep river, very soft in the
bottom, with high banks on either side. There was only one
place to cross 'and there not above six could go abreast'. At
first, de la Hoguette, writing from Kinsale on July 14, tried to
blame the Irish troops for the collision. 'The Irish troops', he
told the Marquis de Louvois, 'were not only beaten; they were
driven before the enemy like sheep'. But, he admitted, bad
generalship lost the battle. Three days later, from Galway, de la
Hoguette gave a more accurate account, saying that 'Tyrconnell retired in good order—it was only when the two retir-

ing bodies came into contact at Duleek that confusion ensued'.

Colonel Conrad von Zurlauben, a veteran who fought under the Vicomte de Turenne, was more blunt. A Swiss German, whose 'Blue' regiment comprised mainly Germans and Swiss, Zurlauben wrote a report 'actuated solely by regard for the King's service'. In that report he said he would expose 'the faults which are the true cause of our losing the battle'. In no uncertain terms Zurlauben claimed that Lauzun, de la Hoguette, and other French officers such as Chémerault, Mérode and Famechon abandoned them. The French colonels, says Zurlauben, put their regimental colours in their pockets and stole away from the battle. His regiment, together with the Irish cavalry, covered the retreat. The infantry retreating from Oldbridge and the troops from Rosnaree reached Duleek at the same time. Some Irish foot came on the Blue regiment in a defile and threatened to break their formation. Zurlauben reported that he had to fire on the panicking soldiers to keep them from destroying the formation of his men and enable them to draw up on the high ground beyond the Duleek crossing. It is significant that of all Louis XIV's own officers serving at the Boyne, Conrad von Zurlauben was the only one invited to Versailles to receive the French king's personal thanks.

Berwick was retreating towards Duleek with the cavalry from Oldbridge, the last Jacobite troops to leave the Boyne area.

'A detachment of the enemy followed us,' he wrote. 'Every time we halted at a defile they did the same. Nay, I believe they were glad to build us a golden bridge.' It is strange that Berwick echoes the words of the Danish ambassador, de la Fouleresse. 'Indeed, this inactivity may have been the result of the death of the Marshal Schomberg who had fallen in the hand to hand fight at Oldbridge. For without injustice to the Prince of Orange, one may assert that Schomberg was the better general. However that may be, the enemy allowed us to retreat peacefully.'

The incident with Zurlauben was over by the time the Duke of Berwick reached Duleek and the crossing. It is strange how history repeats itself for Duleek had been the scene of the aftermath of a battle once before. The bodies of Brian Boru, High King of Ireland, and his son Moragh, slain at the battle of Clontarf in 1014, were brought here by the Monks of the Sword to Duleek Abbey, which had been founded in 488 by St. Cianan.

Then the bodies of the slain High King and his son were taken on to Louth.

'I came up with my cavalry', recalled Berwick, 'just as the last of the King's troops were passing the brook, but those of the Prince of Orange's which kept advancing came up at the same time, so that I was obliged to pass the defile at full speed, and in great disorder, we rallied on the other side, and our whole army was drawn up in line of battle. The enemy did the same opposite us but they did not attack us.' The Jacobite retreat continued another seven miles towards Naul. Most of the Jacobite troops were without direction from the general officers. O'Kelly maintains that in spite of this seeming abandonment the discipline of the bulk of the army still held. '. . . though abandoned by their chief, the cavalry, however, with the assistance of 6,000 French foot made a brave retreat, fighting and marching by day and night till they came to Dublin.'

The pride of the Jacobite infantry, the Grand Prior's regiment, was now being gathered into a disciplined force by Brigadier John Wauchope, in whose brigade it originally had been. Stevens says that he, 'being the oldest lieutenant present', commanded the second division of shot, a company, but as they marched on, the soldiers, still panicking, began to disperse. 'We held onto our march all day, our men dispersing in such manner that we could hardly keep twenty with the colours.' Refugees from other regiments began to join up with them, among them some of Dongan's dragoons. The soldiers were a sorry sight. 'Some had lost their arms (weapons), others their coats, others their hats and shoes and generally everyone carried horror and consternation in his face.' Stevens was bitter.

Whether treason, cowardice, or ill conduct had the greatest share in the shame and losses of this day, with many remains in dispute, nor can be decided by me, not being privy to the counsels nor in a post to see all particulars or be a competent judge of the actions of the generals. The soldier blamed the officer, the officer the general, some were accused as traitors, others as unskilful of their duty, but the greatest imputation was want of valour. But if it be lawful for me to give my sentiments on the matter, in my opinion much may be laid upon mismanagement but much more upon cowardice, and am apt to believe all clamour of treason was raised by some who had given the most eminent signs of fear to cover them and the general disgrace.

The young Duke of Berwick now emerged as the senior officer present and he took command of the retreating troops.

Five miles from Dublin he eventually allowed the weary men to halt in some fields. Stevens noted that 'grief (though the greatest) was not my only burden, marching from three in the morning afoot till dark night, the excessive heat of the sun, and a burning thirst proceeding from the aforesaid cause, which was so vehement I could not quench it though drinking at every ditch and puddle, were altogether sufficient to have conquered a much stronger body'.

Behind them, nearer Duleek, some Jacobite artillery was still functioning and was probably manned by the French who brought it into action against the pursuing troops. Gideon Bonnivert wrote that 'they fired for an hour and a half, small shot, very thick upon us, for they had hid partly in the bushes . . . at last our cannon came and played very smartly upon them till the night coming, they retired, and so did we. We lay in the ploughed lands and had no tents.'

Bellingham had accompanied William and the Dutch cavalry almost as far as Naul when, it being about ten o'clock, dusk began to settle. He acted as William's guide back to the village of Duleek and left him there. 'I returned to Oldbridge, having left the King in his coach at Duleek where he stayed the night. I was almost faint for want of drink and meat.' Story says the Jacobite 'confusion, however, was so great that they left a great many arms and a considerable quantity of ammunition in that village of Duleek, and, indeed, all the country over; but our men were so foolish as to blow up the powder wherever they met with it.'

James' baggage was found at Duleek and the fact that it was there should have been enough to quash the rumours that James had planned to flee before the battle. It was said that he had sent Sir Patrick Trant a full seven days before to secure a ship for him and that his baggage was sent to the boat the evening before the battle. In fact, no such ship was waiting for James when he eventually did decide to leave the country. However, Williamite propaganda tried to build up a picture of James deciding to flee almost as soon as William had landed in Ireland. It was a ridiculous rumour but eagerly accepted by the Williamites. Jacob Hop, the Dutch envoy extraordinary from the States-General, reported that at Duleek the Williamites found guns, baggage, gold watches and silver dinner services as well as numbers of pikes, said to be between 4,000 and 5,000, which the

soldiers burnt to keep them warm, it being a chilly night. Some
of the papers of Tyrconnell were captured and when these were
examined it was reported that they contained details of an
assassination plot against William. Tyrconnell was writing to
Mary of Modena at St. Germain and looked on all as lost. He
ended: 'I have now no hope in anything but in the Jones'
business.' Burnet says that the Marquis of Carmarthen told him
that Jones was an Irishman who had served in France and
Holland, and was chosen to assassinate William. Sir Robert
Southwell had given Burnet copies of the letters found in Tyrconnell's baggage. These reported that Jones, a pseudonym
for a certain Irish soldier, had arrived in Ireland from France
but was making high demands for his services 'if anything can
be high for such a service', adds Tyrconnell. In another letter
Jones is said to have discussed the plot with James 'who did not
like the thing at first. . . . We have now so satisfied him both in
conscience and honour that everything is done as Jones' desires'.
There is no proof that Jones ever attempted his assassination
scheme and whether James' flight from Ireland after the Boyne
made Jones abandon the idea is a matter of conjecture.

Before retiring for the night William called the Duke of
Würtemberg-Neustadt to his carriage, a special sleeping carriage designed by Sir Christopher Wren in which William always
slept during the Irish campaign. He complimented the duke 'on
the bravery of those under his command and praised their good
conduct'. William made sure that the Danish ambassador reported this act in his next letter to Christian V. It would help
Christian maintain the Danish troops in William's service. Then
William sent for the Count Schomberg to commiserate with
him on his father's death. 'I deeply lament your father', he told
the Count, 'for I had a sincere friendship for him. I shall never
forget his services nor yours. I owe this day to you and will
remember it all my life. You have lost much in your father.
But I shall be your father, your's and your children's.'

Most of William's officers lay in the fields with their men,
without the luxury of a coach. Captain Rowland Davies wrote:
'It being very dark we were forced to be in the field all night
with our horses in our hands.' George Clarke, the Secretary
at War, who had attached himself to some dragoons chasing
the Jacobite cavalry, noted: 'We shifted as well as we could
without tents or servants, and slept very heartily upon the

ground. In the night the enemy's horse that faced our dragoons marched away and we heard no more of them.'

For the Danish ambassador the fight was over. 'Several deserters, or perhaps people who have not been able to keep up with the hasty march of the enemy, have informed us that it is King James' intention to collect together the remains of his army before the gates of Dublin, and to oppose the King once more before yielding up the capital. This seems to be a mere conjecture, and is void of all probability.'

Sir Thomas Bellingham rode back to the camp at Oldbridge, exhausted but happy. 'A joyful day', he wrote in his diary before rolling up in a blanket to sleep.

CHAPTER 3

THE FLIGHT

'others coming in dusty and weary'

The inhabitants of Dublin had been 'wakened very early this Tuesday morning by an alarm and the news that there would be a battle' says the 'Person of Quality'. Simon Luttrell and Denis MacGillicuddy, commanding the city, gave orders that the gates of Dublin were to be kept shut at all times. The Williamite sympathisers in the town, of which there were a great many, kept in their houses behind locked and barred doors and awaited the news 'with the greatest apprehension'. Every hour rumours flew through the city. One had it that a French fleet under Admiral Tourville had entered Dublin Bay, another that the French had captured the Isle of Wight and were now marching on Dover. A third rumour said an important French messenger had landed at Waterford. Then there was the story that the right wing of William's army had been crushingly defeated and pursued from the field and that William had been taken prisoner. 'But', says the 'Person of Quality', 'at five that afternoon, some that had made their escape on tired horses told us the Irish were much worsted, and others at six, that they were totally defeated, from hence, till one that night, all the entrances of the town were filled with dusty, wounded and tired soldiers, and carriages perpetually coming in. We saw several of King James' Horse Guards coming in, straggling without pistols or swords, and could not tell what was become of him.'

The stream of weary soldiers, many of the officers in carriages, made a constant flow into the city until well after midnight. It was 'nearer ten that night' that James rode into the city accompanied by two hundred of Sarsfield's horse regiment 'all in disorder'. The Williamite sympathisers 'concluded now that it was a total rout and that the enemy were just ready to come into the town'. They were greatly surprised, however, when, an hour or two later, 'we heard the whole body of the Irish horse coming in, in very good order, with kettle drums, hautboys and trumpets'. These regiments were the ones which had been at Rosnaree and had not taken part in the battle.

James was reported to have entered Dublin in a silent and dejected condition. 'In a manner stunned', observed one reporter. A popular tale was told that Lady Tyrconnell had asked the dejected King James what he would like to eat, to which James is said to have replied that after the breakfast that he had had, he had little stomach for his supper. Some years later another tale was spread that James had greeted Lady Tyrconnell with the bitter remark: 'Your countrymen, madam, can run well.' To which Lady Tyrconnell had replied: 'Not so well as your majesty, for I see you have won the race.'

James sent for those of his Privy Councillors who were still in the capital and asked them for their comments on Lauzun's advice that he should leave for France to avoid falling into the hands of the Williamites. Sir Richard Nagle, William Herbert (the Duke of Powis), Lord Gosworth and Sir Ignatius White, whose French title was the Marquis d'Albeville, listened to the proposal with their minds already full of plans for their own safety. Naturally they agreed to evacuate the city from the advancing Williamites. James saw a Major Wilson, who had just arrived from France, the source of the rumour of the 'important French messenger from Waterford'. He had brought some letters from Mary of Modena. James read the letters which gave news of the Duke of Luxembourg's defeat of the Dutch in Flanders. James says the Queen suggested that he should leave William in Ireland and return to France to organise an army which he could land in England in William's absence. It seems a strange proposal for Mary of Modena to put forward for she could not have known that, the day before, the Anglo–Dutch fleet had been decisively smashed off Beachy Head by the French, thus leaving the sea routes wide open for an invasion of England. But James, when he came to write his memoirs, made this his main reason for deciding to leave Ireland.

At midnight, a rider from the Duke of Berwick arrived to say that he had rallied seven thousand infantry and was encamped at Brasil, just out of Dublin. He now had his own regiment intact together with Maxwell's and Purcell's dragoons, but he needed more cavalry to protect the infantry from any Williamite attack.

James despatched three troops of Lord Abercorn's horse and six troops of Simon Luttrell's dragoons to join his son. Berwick's brother, Henry Fitzjames, had arrived in the city with a hundred men of the King's Horse Guards. Soon after, Tyrconnell's chaplain Father Taafe galloped into Dublin with a message that Tyrconnell 'begged His Majesty would not remain an instant in Dublin but would repair to France with all possible expedition, and would send all the troops that were in the city to Leixlip to meet M. de Lauzun and himself, because they did not mean to march so far as Dublin for fear they should not have sufficient time to draw off their tired forces'. Tyrconnell and Lauzun had contacted Berwick and wanted all available troops to assemble at Leixlip, ten miles west of Dublin on the Liffey. Tyrconnell's entreaty to the King to leave the country was reinforced by a note from Lauzun.

Before five o'clock, after a few hours rest, James was up and had summoned the Lord Mayor, Terence McDermott, and some others who had remained in the city. All through the night the principal Jacobites had been seized with panic and many families were crowding the roads, fleeing westwards. James was bitter. Everything, he told the officials gathered before him, was against him. In England he had an army which would have fought if they had not proved false. In Ireland the soldiers, generally, were loyal enough but the people would not stand by him. Of his army at the Boyne, he said: 'When it came to a trial, they basely fled the field and left the spoil to the enemy, nor could they be prevailed upon to rally, though their loss in the whole defeat was but inconsiderable; so that henceforth I never determined to head an Irish army and do now resolve to shift myself, and so, gentlemen, must you.' He added that they must not take vengeance on any Williamites or Protestants, nor were they to plunder or set fire to Dublin 'in which he had an interest'.

Just after five o'clock James, with his son Henry Fitzjames and the Duke of Powis, mounted their horses. At that moment the French officers, de la Hoguette, Chémerault, Famechon and Mérode, arrived on exhausted horses and demanded fresh mounts to accompany the King. There were none to be had and James, not wishing to delay further, set off towards Bray with a hundred troopers of his Horse Guards.

Five miles outside of Dublin Berwick's camp was stirring in

William attempting to lead the Dutch cavalry across the Boyne.
Aquatint by J. Grozer after B. West, 1771

William III entering Dublin on Sunday, 6 July, 1690.
... ... published by A. Schoonebeek, 1690

The River Boyne at Rosnaree, at the spot where Count Meinhard Schomberg began his feint attack, crossing with a division of 10,000 men and opposed by Sir Neil O'Neil's 480 dragoons.

An Paipread as Tpein

Oh Patrick Sarsfield, Ireland's Wonder
Who fought in the fields like any thunder
One of king James's chief Commanders
In the flood of crows in Flanders

Muire Jarm Calasgaid An

PATRICK SARSFIELD EARL OF   LUCAN, VISCOUNT OF TULLY,
BARON OF ROSBERRY, & COLONEL   OF THE LIFE GUARDS TO JAMES
THE SECOND, COMMANDER   CHIEF OF THE FORCES IN IRE:
LAND, AND AFTERWARDS GE   RAL OFFICER IN THE FRENCH SER
VICE. KILLED IN THE BAT   OF NEERWINDE, OR LANDEN.

Patrick Sarsfield, Major-General of cavalry for James at the Boyne.
Engraving by M. A. Bregeon

the early morning light. John Stevens was woken to the quick beat of the reveille. 'At the break of day those few drums beat as formerly as if we had a considerable body, but it was only mere form and we scarce had the shadows of regiments, the bodies being dispersed and gone.' Berwick moved part of his horse straight towards Leixlip while Brigadier Wauchope posted himself north of Dublin, straddling the road, to divert troops towards the west. The rest of the infantry marched towards Dublin in 'hopes', says Stevens, 'of gathering part of the scattered herd'. Just before Dublin the regiments were halted in some fields and the standards of each regiment were raised, 'that all stragglers might know within to repair'. Some three hours later the regiments had been more respectfully reinforced.

The 'Person of Quality' was abroad early and saw just after dawn 'the French and a great party of Irish foot' entering the city. 'These being a little rested, marched out again to meet the enemy, which were supposed to draw nigh.' The town was still in an uproar as Jacobite refugees started to pour west towards Limerick. The 'Person of Quality' recalled:

All this day, being Wednesday, we saw nothing in this town but officers and carriages, and the principal persons of the town, their wives and families going away; others coming in dusty and weary, and getting away as fast as they could; the gates were still kept by the militia, and the Castle by 250 of the Governor's foot soldiers who still threatened that before they left the town they would burn and plunder us. This of a long time had been their talk though King James said it was a report raised by Protestants to make him odious. Yet some Irish persons of note advised their Protestant friends a few days before this to leave the town because they would not be safe here.

Tyrconnell and Lauzun arrived later that morning to find James gone and confusion and panic in the city. Wauchope told them that the King had left instructions that the Jacobite army must make either for Limerick or Kinsale. Lauzun, writing to Seignelay, says they decided the most advantageous position was Limerick and orders to rendezvous there were passed to the scattered Jacobite regiments.

Stevens, with the remnants of what had been four regiments, marched into the city about ten o'clock, through the outskirts and across the river at Bloody Bridge, the site of the modern Rory O'More Bridge, 'which is the farthest off in the suburbs'. The bridge had been named after a riot which had taken place on it when it was first built. The regiments halted in a field 'at Kilmainham, a hamlet adjoining the city'. The general opinion amongst the officers was that the regiments should camp in Kilmainham Park until they received reinforcements, whereupon they should join Simon Luttrell's forces in defending the city from Williamite attack. By noon, however, orders came for three of the regiments to march to Leixlip and Stevens found his own Grand Prior's regiment had been deserted by the rest of the officers and 'reduced to only twenty men with the colours'. He decided to accept total responsibility and lead his men after the others towards Naas, to the south-west. On the road, the twenty survivors of the Grand Prior's regiment overtook the regiment of Dominic Sarsfield, the fifth Viscount Kilmallock, whose regiment had been stationed in Dublin during the battle. When Stevens came upon it, it was marching in good order along the road, its 720 men equipped and rested with its colonel, lieutenant-colonel, major, nine captains, thirteen lieutenants and twelve ensigns, plus its surgeon and chaplain making a very brave display. Among the lieutenants of the regiment was Hugolín (Little Hugo) Spenser, the grandson of Edmund Spenser, the famous Elizabethan poet. Spenser had been a colonist in Munster in Elizabeth's day and had deplored how many colonists were adopting the language and manners of the 'mere Irish'. He would have turned in his grave, such was his hatred of the native Irish, had he known that Hugolín, adopting even an Irish form of his name, was to become an officer in 'an Irish Papist regiment'. To heighten the irony, another grandson had been banished west of the Shannon as an 'Irish Papist' during the Cromwellian colonisation.

Stevens and his men marched at the back of Lord Kilmallock's regiment until they were within two miles of Naas. Rumours and false alarms as to the nearness of William's troops were rife. Two miles from Naas a galloper told Kilmallock that the Williamites were close behind. Kilmallock's officers attempted to get their men into ambush positions behind the hedges on either side of the road but, says Stevens, 'the confusion and terror of the soldiers who had never seen the enemy was such they were forced in all haste to march away'. No enemy was within twenty miles of them but 'fear never *thinks* itself out of danger' observed Stevens. 'We followed Kilmallock's regiment with such speed it had been hard for an enemy to overtake us, and that regiment though till then untouched was in such consternation that when they came to Naas they were not one hundred strong.'

Lieutenant-Colonel O'Donnell, who was in Naas, took command of the survivors of the Grand Prior's regiment. Stevens says he tried to persuade O'Donnell that the men needed rest and that, as they had marched two days without food, he should get them some quarters to stay and some provisions, 'but all in vain'. 'The general infection had seized him,' says Stevens. 'And he fancied each minute he stayed was to him time lost and an opportunity given to the enemy to gain ground on us. Therefore, following the dictates of his fear, he hastened away, commanding all to follow him, but necessity pressing more than his usurped authority, I stayed awhile in the town with an ensign who had a lame horse . . .' Stevens and the ensign managed to get a loaf, which they ate, and feeling more comfortable they both mounted the lame horse and set off in the wake of the retreating soldiers. They reached Kilcullen, standing by the River Liffey, 'where we could hear no news of our men'. It was nearly dusk now so the two officers found the deserted ruins of an old house where they fell asleep.

After Stevens had left Dublin, at about four o'clock, the Irish horse regiments which had been withdrawn from the city towards Leixlip returned, followed by the French and Irish foot. 'Presently', says the 'Person of Quality', 'a buzz ran through the town that it was going to be burnt.' A number of Jacobites who had sought refuge with Williamite sympathisers panicked and rushed out to declare their loyalty to James again but 'all these forces marched through the town without doing any injury and were drawn up by Lord Tyrconnell on the other side of it'.

The six thousand militia troops followed and Simon Luttrell and MacGillicuddy started to form their guard up. Some 2,300 prominent Williamite prisoners were gathered outside Dublin Castle, guarded by foot soldiers under Luttrell's command. Luttrell told the prisoners that he was going to take them as hostages. At that moment a cry rang out that the Williamites had landed at Dublin harbour. It was now dusk and Luttrell, realising it would take too long to move 2,300 prisoners, seized only the most important of them and marched out after the rest of the Jacobite troops.

For the moment, Dublin was silent. Had the Jacobites really gone? After a little while some more adventurous souls went to Dublin Castle and found the grim thirteenth-century fortress in the hands of Captain Farlow, the Williamite soldier who had been captured during the skirmish at Moyry Pass. Farlow had released Captain Robert Fitzgerald, an uncle of Wentworth Fitzgerald, the seventeenth Earl of Kildare, who had been turned out of the army by Tyrconnell. Farlow and Fitzgerald suggested that a militia be formed and the houses of several Jacobites were raided for arms. The militia were to prevent the Jacobites from setting fire to the city until William's army could march into it. The 'Person of Quality' records that some of the former prisoners from Galway 'and some other rabble committed outrages in taking arms'. The former prisoners wanted revenge on the Jacobites or on any that were denounced as Jacobite sympathisers. Both Farlow and Fitzgerald tried to prevent looting and on one occasion, when Fitzgerald found a mob breaking into Patrick Sarsfield's house, 'he was forced to exercise his authority with cane and sword'. Fitzgerald was up most of the night dealing with looters and arsonists. A French soldier was caught in Kevin Street trying to set fire to the thatch of the houses and was imprisoned in the Castle. He was not executed because he was doing it under orders from his major. By midnight on July 2 the Jacobite army had quit Dublin and it was in the hands of a poorly armed militia.

In the meantime, James and his bodyguard had reached Bray, thirteen miles south of Dublin, riding their horses at a quick canter. The bridge across the Dargle River was the main gateway into the Wicklow Mountains and James, rather surprisingly, ordered his Horse Guards to remain at the bridge and guard it until noon. He then went on with a small entourage through the mountains but kept fairly near the coast, past Wicklow itself and through the Vale of Avoca towards Arklow. James recalls he rested for an hour or two at 'the house of a gentleman of the name of Hatchet near Arklow'.

Hugh Howard, a brother of the first Viscount Wicklow, was to record exactly a hundred years later a story told to him as a youth by an old man called Richard Johnson 'who was son to the gardener at Shelton'.

. . . just after the Battle of the Boyne, being then a young boy, as he was standing one evening in company with a labouring man of the name of

Coghlan in Shelton avenue (this must have been the evening of July 2, 1690) he saw two tall gentlemen, grandly mounted and all covered with dust, ride down Stringers Hill on their way to the ford, but instead of proceeding onwards, they turned up the avenue whither he followed them, not knowing who they were. When they came to the house, which was then in possession of one Mr Hatchet (he was the sequestrator) they alighted and sat down in the porch, where they had some cold meat and a jug of strong beer. While they continued there which was only for a few minutes, one of them was seized with a violent bleeding of the nose, which stained the post of that side of the porch where the gentleman sat. When the bleeding was stopped they mounted their horses again, and rode down the avenue and across the ford (probably the short cut to Duncannon Ford). He afterwards knew for certain that person whose nose had bled, was King James II, and that the other was a person of distinction. The porch was afterwards taken down and the post with the blood on it (which I have seen) long carefully preserved but has been since burned by the carelessness of servants.

Significantly, it may also be noted that at a previous point of stress, at Salisbury in 1688, James was also afflicted by a violent nose bleed. James was, however, accompanied by more than one 'person of distinction' and it seems odd that he should have ridden up to the house with only one other companion, though it could well be that the others had gone on to reconnoitre a way across the Derry Water.

James was now heading for Enniscorthy. The King's party were not two miles on the road when they were overtaken by the four French officers, de la Hoguette, Chémerault, Mérode and Famechon. They were breathless and cried that the Williamites were close behind. They were, of course, still north of Dublin. Was de la Hoguette obeying the instructions of Lauzun to ensure James left Ireland and did not change his mind? Or had he mistakenly thought James' Horse Guards, left guarding the bridge at Bray, miles away, were Williamite troopers? Certainly, they were not military men. Chémerault, for example, was merely a gentleman usher to the Dauphiness. It seems certain that Lauzun had charged de la Hoguette with the mission of getting James out of the country before he had second thoughts.

James' party reached Enniscorthy and demanded fresh horses from a Quaker named Francis Randall. Randall, who provided the horses, noted that the King was riding with his pistols at full cock, a very dangerous thing to do.

It was nearly dawn on Thursday, July 3, when James and his party reached Duncannon. James rested here most of the day while de la Hoguette rode up to Passage, higher on the Suir, and found anchored there a St. Malo privateer mounting twenty-five guns and ironically called the *Lauzun*. The captain dropped down river with the tide towards evening, picking up James opposite Duncannon. By nightfall the ship had rounded Hook Head and was standing out to sea. The next morning, following James' instructions, the *Lauzun* put into the port of Kinsale, at the mouth of the river Brandon in Co. Cork, where just over a year before James had been greeted so rapturously. At Kinsale James sat down to write some final instructions to Tyrconnell, informing him that he was now viceroy and in sole command in Ireland. He was to continue to fight or make terms with William as he saw fit. Further, James was sending him 50,000 pistoles, all the money he had available. A French pistole, a gold coin, was worth six shillings sterling. Having completed his final orders James went on board the flagship of M. du Quesne's squadron of three frigates. These vessels were protecting seven merchantmen which had just arrived in Kinsale laden with corn and wine for the Jacobites. Within a few hours, towards midday on Friday, July 4, 1690, James left Ireland.

'the enemy made but a poor fight of it'

Sir Thomas Bellingham states that the bulk of the Williamite army on July 2 'stayed all this day at Duleek'. The only excitement came when six troops of Jacobite horse and three regiments of foot appeared on the Williamite flank at Duleek. Captain Rowland Davies, who had returned to the village, said that the Jacobites, not learning of the defeat of their army, had been marching up from Munster to join James' main body. They sent two soldiers to find out who the great concourse of soldiers in and around Duleek were. The Williamites promptly seized the unfortunate men and hanged them. The Jacobites then withdrew with a marked swiftness.

The main action of the day was at the town of Drogheda where Brigadier de la Mellonière, with 1,000 horse and 300 foot plus eight field guns, had gone to demand the surrender of the garrison, Lord Iveagh's foot regiment and some horse amounting to 1,300 Jacobite soldiers. The safety of Drogheda had been entrusted to Brian Magennis, the fifth Viscount Iveagh, but he seems to have fled westward leaving the city in the care of Brigadier William Tuite. Tuite had received de la Mellonière's first summons to surrender his garrison with disdain. De la Mellonière sent a more forceful demand stating that if he was forced to fire his cannon on Drogheda no quarter would be given. Tuite was pressed by the anxious towns people, many of whom still had horrific memories of the day, forty-one years before, when the town had similarly been summoned to surrender by Oliver Cromwell. The memory of how Cromwell carried out his threat and how 3,500 of their relatives, friends and neighbours had been slain and others shipped off to slavery in the Barbados was still a vivid one. Tuite now sent back a messenger asking for terms but if de la Mellonière wanted an unconditional surrender he would defend Drogheda 'to the last extremity'. De la Mellonière replied that his orders were to disarm the garrison and that the Jacobites could march out without arms, provided they quickly resolved whether to accept the offer. In the meantime de la Mellonière erected his gun batteries, placing his field guns in two positions ready for a bombardment of the town. The capitulation was agreed about mid-morning of July 3 and signed by Tuite and counter-signed by the French commander. The Danish ambassador sent a copy to Christian V with his letter dated July 8. The Jacobite officers were allowed to keep their swords and the garrison marched out towards Athlone. With no hostile garrison at his rear William could now move forward towards Dublin. The terms had been liberal, purposefully so, in order to quicken an end to the campaign. An English regiment occupied Drogheda while de la Mellonière rejoined the main army. The English officers, says Story, 'took great care to preserve the town from the violence of the soldiers'. Drogheda, in view of its past treatment at the hands of the English, was to be treated with kid gloves so that the Irish would not feel their situation to be hopeless, and this cause them to hold out in desperation.

Wednesday, July 2, was a day of ease for the soldiers of William's main force. They could sit back and take stock of the situation, assess the casualties and plan ahead. The casualties were few by comparison with other major engagements. Robert Parker wrote: 'I have met with several accounts of the battle, some of them very particular in reciting all the charges and repulses that had been made on both sides, as if it had lasted the greatest part of the day, and the field had been covered with the slain. But, after all, the enemy made but a poor fight of it, as may appear by the loss on both sides. The enemy had not quite 800 slain and about as many taken. And we not above 500 killed and as many wounded.'

Bellingham concluded that 2,000 Jacobites had been killed and only 200 Williamites. Narcissus Luttrell, on receiving the despatches from Duleek on July 7 in London, claimed that some 3,000 Jacobites had died. He noted in his journal: 'King James did not engage at all in this action . . . but was upon a hill at some distance; and when he saw how it went, he returned to Dublin, and stayed there that night, and the next morning early, left the city and went towards Waterford declaring he would never trust an Irish army any more.'

Story estimated between 1,000 and 1,500 Jacobites killed and 'nigh 400' Williamites. The *Villare Hibernicum* says the dead on both sides were 'not above 1,600' together. The Jacobite *Light to the Blind* says that only 500 Jacobites had been killed and 1,000 Williamites. The Danish division were more precise in their estimation of their own casualty list: twenty-four cavalry troopers and four foot soldiers dead and twenty-two cavalry troopers and twenty-one foot soldiers wounded—surprisingly low figures for their encounter across Yellow Island. The 'Person of Quality' wrote:

I am told by one that viewed the dead that there was not above 1,000 killed on both sides, though perhaps you may hear of greater numbers, which is a wonderful thing, that so small a loss should disperse the whole Irish army, who seemed to be blown away only by a wind from God; the main body of them is supposed to be about Limerick, but the opposition they will give will depend very much on the success of the Fleets.

Overall, it would seem that the most likely estimate is probably about 500 Williamite soldiers killed and nearly 1,000 Jacobites. Würtemberg-Neustadt adds that 'several hundred common soldiers' of the Jacobite army were taken prisoner.

So July 2 was a day of writing reports and letters. The Danish ambassador, 'writing in haste on a drum and not at all at my ease', told Christian V that because of the haste 'it is therefore possible that I have omitted a few particulars or a few circumstances. This I shall remedy by the next post.' But because 'the King intends sending a messenger to England today with the important news of the engagement which took place yesterday and which opens the way for the easy conquest of the Kingdom, I was unwilling to lose this opportunity of sending this report to your Majesty'.

Certainly the Williamites overestimated the importance of the battle in the short term. De la Fouleresse had felt it 'opens the way for the easy conquest' of Ireland and his optimism was shared by Würtemberg-Neustadt writing three days later to Jens Harboe, the Danish Chief Secretary of War. 'At last King James' army has been routed in its camp in spite of the difficulty encountered . . . the enemy are completely scattered and it appears that the war in Ireland will soon be over.' Jacob Hop, the Dutch envoy, sat down and wrote his account of the battle for the States-General which they published later in the month in *Europishe Mercurius*. Sir Robert Southwell wrote to his friend Daniel Finch, the second Earl of Nottingham, about the battle and Nottingham immediately took the letter to Queen Mary. Mary immediately sat down and drafted off a message to her husband expressing her joy but 'I must put you in mind of one thing, believing it now the season, which is, that you take care of the church in Ireland. Everybody agrees that it is the worst in Christendom.' The official account of the battle was drafted by Hans Willem Bentinck and copies were sent to England and Holland for publication as a *Narrative of the Fight at the Boyne*.

Although, as the author of *Light to the Blind* pointed out, in terms of the battles yet to be fought by the Grand Alliance, the Boyne was hardly more than 'a mere skirmish', the fact that it precipitated the flight of James was a tremendous victory for William. No one saw this more clearly than the Dutch commander, Godart van Ginkel, who wrote to his father observing: 'This is a great victory, which will do good throughout Europe and give great satisfaction to the allies.'

During the evening of July 2, Captain Rowland Davies noted that one William Sanders had arrived from Dublin in the Williamite camp bringing with him the news that James had fled to the coast on his way to France.

'*we now perceived ourselves at liberty*'

At six o'clock on the morning of Thursday, July 3, a crowd of gentlemen gathered in one of the state rooms in Dublin Castle. As chairman they elected Anthony Dopping, the Anglican Bishop of Meath who, when Christ Church had been seized and consecrated to Catholic use in September of the previous year, had remonstrated with James and demanded its return to the Anglican Church. James had replied with a half apology saying that had he been in Dublin at the time it would not have been taken away, but since it was, it could not be restored without annoying the Irish Catholics 'whose interest was all he had to trust to'. St. Patrick's Cathedral and a number of other Dublin Anglican churches were similarly seized but, by February of that year, they had all been given back with the exception of Christ Church. James had issued a proclamation forbidding the seizure by Catholics of Anglican churches. The Anglicans praised the Bishop of Meath for managing to obtain this proclamation. They were not surprised when he was thrown into prison, along with other leading Protestants and Williamite supporters, soon after William's landing in Belfast.

The gentlemen of Dublin had a problem. The Hon. Robert Fitzgerald, hollow-eyed and fatigued after a sleepless night moving around the city with his makeshift militia in an attempt to stop looters, arsonists and rioteers, told the meeting that the city was getting out of hand. He, Captain Farlow, Captain Slaughter and Sir Robert Gore had done their best to prevent disorders but although most of the Jacobite administration had left the city with their families there were still many left, beseiged in their houses by hoards of prowling pro-Williamites. Similarly, many of the houses abandoned by the Jacobites were being ransacked by mobs and although he had done his best, the few men he had and the fewer arms were not enough to guard the city until William's army arrived, *if*, he emphasised, they did arrive. So far there had been no word from the victorious Williamites and the Jacobites could well return to the city at any time.

The gentlemen agreed that the Bishop of Meath and Dr. William King, the dean of St. Patrick's, should head a committee which would take charge of the safety of the city. The committee was quickly instituted and promptly voted that the tired Fitzgerald should be the acting governor of the city. A proclamation to this effect was sent out by beat of drum to call the people to order and beg them not to commit excesses against anyone they suspected of being Jacobite in sympathy. A message was also sent out post haste to William, telling him that the Jacobites had fled the town and that Dublin was not fortified against him. Fitzgerald added a note addressed to the nearest Williamite commander asking for troops to be sent immediately to the city as the Protestant 'rabble' were getting out of control and either they or the Jacobites, who could well return, might set fire to the city.

On the same morning the Williamite army broke camp around Duleek and, according to Captain Rowland Davies, marched to a place within two miles of Swords and set up camp again. He recorded that some three hundred Dubliners came out to congratulate William and assure him that James had fled. It was here that William received Fitzgerald's plea for assistance. 'I see I have some good friends in Dublin and am much obliged to Mr. Fitzgerald,' William told the messenger. 'I will take care to send some horses as soon as I can and desire he will go on taking care of the place as he has done.' When the messenger arrived back at Dublin Castle to tell Fitzgerald that the Williamite troops were now on the way, the pro-Williamites were jubilant. An anonymous Williamite supporter wrote: 'There was very great joy, and sorrow and sadness was gone away, when we crept out of our houses and found ourselves, as it were, in a new world.'

Sir Thomas Bellingham and a troop of dragoons were ordered to ride for Dublin and take charge of the Castle, putting themselves at the disposal of Fitzgerald and the new council. Bellingham was also asked to make an inventory of what provisions were available to the Williamite army in Dublin. James Butler, the second Duke of Ormonde, who had been condemned to inaction as the commander of William's English Horse Guard at the Boyne, was ordered to take nine troops of horse into Dublin the next morning. Ormonde was eager at the chance of some possible action and probably just as eager to see Dublin Castle where he had been born some twenty-five years earlier. To support Ormonde's troops William also ordered Count Henry Nassau, Lord Auverquerque, to take two battalions of his Dutch Blue Guards.

'Till afternoon this Thursday,' wrote the 'Person of Quality', 'we did not hear a word of the English army; meantime we had reports that the Irish and French were coming back, and very near us, which gave a damp to our briskness; but this blowing over, and the certain account of the English army being come, we now perceived ourselves at liberty.'

The troop of dragoons entered Dublin at eight o'clock that evening to a great clamour from the pro-Williamite citizens who almost dragged the soldiers off their horses in joy. Bellingham went to Dublin Castle to report to the council and then went off to stay the night with his 'cousin Croker'. *Villare Hibernicum* recorded: 'At eight o'clock this night one troop of dragoons came as guard to an officer that came to take charge of the stores. It was impossible that the King himself, coming after this, could be welcomed with equal joy as this one troop: the Protestants hung about the horses and were ready to pull the men off them, as they marched up to the Castle.' The French trooper Gideon Bonnivert missed the excitement of the entry into Dublin. He wrote in his journal: 'Thursday, being the third of July, we came near a fine house, belonging to a Papist, where we encamped, and where I fell sick of a violent fever.'

Some miles to the south, at Kilcullen, Stevens and his ensign companion 'were roused out of a dead sleep' by 'a great number of dragoons and others riding through the town as fast as their horses could carry them, and crying the enemy was within a mile of them'. Mounting their solitary lame horse, they rode some five or six miles when they were overtaken by Lord Tyrconnell himself, riding in a coach with his family and several bodyguards. Tyrconnell demanded the lame horse for his own entourage and 'they being too strong for us to cope with, for them might was the greatest right' observed a bitter Stevens, 'they carried him away leaving us afoot, weary and without friends or money'.

The two officers trudged on and came to a village. 'Being desperate' they hit on a plan to attack the village, the men being out in the fields, and try to 'force away a horse under the colour of pressing, but in reality was not much better than robbing' admitted Stevens. The two officers ran into the village but the women set up such an outcry that their menfolk arrived, some carrying half pikes, and chased the two dejected men away with curses. Stevens and his comrade plodded on down the road to Athy. 'A great shower of rain falling increased our misfortunes, making the ground slippery. We could scarce draw our tired limbs.' But their luck changed for an officer called Dowdall, whom Stevens knew, and a cornet of Simon Luttrell's dragoons overtook them and mounted the two weary men behind them. In this fashion they rode into Shanganagh, a village a mile from Athy, where the rain forced them to stay until evening.

On the morning of July 4 the Duke of Ormonde and Count Henry Nassau entered Dublin with the cavalry and the Dutch Blue Guards. It was a 'very hot' day, observed Bellingham, who rode back to Swords to give William an 'account of stores and provisions that were in Dublin and twenty miles around. I presented him with a basket of cherries, the first he ate since he came to the kingdom. He took them with his own hand very kindly.'

William had decided to keep his army at Swords for the rest of the day and declared it officially a day of rest for the entire army. Captain Rowland Davies decided to seize the opportunity to ride into Dublin 'to see my Lord Primate whom I found very well and cheerful'. In the afternoon he watched the Dutch Blue Guards taking formal possession of Dublin Castle and the Duke of Ormonde posting guards on the outposts of the city. 'In the evening I went with Frank Burton and some others to The Three Tuns and we lay together at Robert Foulkes' lodging house in Wine Tavern Street.'

In Wexford a Captain Thomas Knox, who had been a prisoner for many months in the jail, learning of the defeat at the Boyne and the entry into Dublin, led a prison break, seized the Jacobite guards and declared himself governor of Wexford for William III.

That morning, in Athy, Stevens found a lieutenant from his regiment from whom he managed to borrow a horse and so set out for Kilkenny which he reached at noon. The town, once the capital of the Irish Catholic Confederacy, where countless Irish parliaments had met, was crowded with troops, all travel weary and hungry, and many wounded. He recalled:

All the shops and public houses in the town were shut and neither meat nor drink to be had, though many were fainting through want and weariness. Hunger and thirst put me forward to seek relief, where nothing but necessity could have carried me, but the invincible power of want hides all blushes, so hearing the stores at the Castle were broke up, and much bread and drink given out, I resolved to try my fortune there and found drink carried out in pails, and many of the rabble drunk with what they had got; yet upon my approach I perceived some officers, whom want had carried thither as well as me, but were somewhat more forward, so ill treated by Brigadier Mackay first and next by the Duke of Tyrconnell, who had a lieutenant thrust in the breast with his cane, that I went away resolved rather to perish than to run the hazard of being ill used.

Stevens searched the town and somehow found 'our colours and some officers'. Apart from these there were no soldiers from the Grand Prior's regiment and 'so the ensigns were ordered to strip their colours, and thus we set out on our way to Limerick'.

The following day, Saturday, William marched his army into a camp at Finglas. It was found that a number of Jacobite soldiers were returning to Dublin to surrender. According to Würtemberg-Neustadt in a letter to Christian V: 'Zurlauben's regiment was badly broken up. A few days ago five hundred, mostly German, came to Dublin, most of them have joined the army. About one hundred have joined Your Majesty's battalions.' Other Jacobite soldiers returned with a more sinister purpose. A number of private soldiers from Sir Michael Creagh's regiment of foot were given permission to remain in Dublin to seek work as porters and colliers. In reality they were acting as agents for the Jacobite army and were not discovered until November when a number of them were arrested and imprisoned.

Sunday, July 6, was, according to Bellingham, 'a hot but gloomy day'. It was the day which William chose to make his triumphal entry into Dublin. The *London Gazette* of July 14 reports that he rode 'in great splendour' to St. Patrick's Cathedral where a Te Deum was sung and 'an excellent sermon' was preached by the Dean, Dr. William King. The 'Person of Quality' who was in the Cathedral with the former mayor, Terence MacDermott, and aldermen, 'heard a sermon preached by Dr. King concerning the power of God of which that which seemed to us greatest upon the earth, mighty armies were a faint shadow'. After which the towns people 'ran about shouting and embracing one another and blessing God for his wonderful deliverance as if they had been alive from the dead; the streets were filled with crowds and shouting and the poor Roman Catholics now lay in the same terrors as we had done some few days before.'

Captain Davies, who preached in the camp at Finglas to the

men of Lord Cavendish's horse regiment, then walked to Dublin to dine with his friend Dean Burgh. He recalled that the city was full of bonfires. George Story also had time to visit Dublin which he found 'is by much the largest and best [city] in all Ireland, and inferior to none in England except London. Most of the houses and streets are very regular and modern and the people as fashionable as anywhere. It is called by Ptolemy, Eblana, and the Irish call'd it Bala Cleirigh, that is the town upon the hurdles, because they said it was built upon a funny, boggy place, but whatever it has been, the ground about it is now very sound and the air wholesome. . . .' Later that evening, after William had returned to Finglas for dinner and issued an order that no soldiers should remain in the city except guards and officers, Captain Davies met up with his colonel and they sat and drank awhile in The Three Tuns in St. Michael's Lane. Davies had to borrow a horse from a Lieutenant Meredith in order to ride back to camp.

The next day, Monday, William received a deputation from the aldermen of Dublin who proposed that they remain in office with the powers to elect others 'to complete their number'. These were Sir Humphrey Jervis, John Desmynieres, John Smith, Philip Castleton, Walter Molley, William Billington, Giles Mee, John Braddock, George Blackhall, William Watts and Michael Mitchell. They proposed that Walter Molley be made Lord Mayor of the city and that Anthony Perkins and Mark Ransford serve him as sheriffs 'until such time as your Majesty's pleasure shall be known'. William consented and appointed Brigadier Trelawny as governor of Dublin with Robert Fitzgerald as constable of Dublin Castle. A special Commission for Securing Rebels' Goods and Estates was set up consisting of nine men, including the Bishop of Meath and Francis Aungier, the first earl of Longford, whose house had been burnt by rioters. They were to be responsible for the final great confiscation by the English of Irish lands for resettlement by English colonists. By the end of the decade some 1,100,000 acres had been seized by the victorious Williamites.

On the same day William issued a royal proclamation from Finglas which began:

As it has pleased Almighty God to bless our army in this kingdom with a late victory over our enemies at the Boyne, and with the possession of our capital city of Dublin, and with the general desperation of all that did oppose us, we are now in so happy a prospect of our affairs and of extinguishing the rebellion of this kingdom, that we hold it reasonable to think of mercy, and to have compassion upon those whom we judge to have been seduced.

He promised his protection to 'all poor labourers, common soldiers, country farmers, ploughmen, colliers, whatsoever, as also all citizens, townsmen, tradesmen and artificers' who remained at home or fled, if they returned by August 1 and surrendered their arms and gave their names for registration 'to such Justices of the Peace as are, or shall be, appointed by us, not only to receive the same but also to register the appearance of such of the persons as shall come in and submit to our authority'. Tenants were to pay rents, especially to Protestant colonial landlords whom they had tried to remove, but in other cases, as regards Catholic landlords, tenants could hold the money until further deliberation was made. All disorders were to be sternly suppressed and the leaders of such disturbances would be shown little mercy unless they showed themselves fully penitent.

As for the 'desperate leaders of the rebellion', they would be left to the fortunes of war unless they showed William that they were deserving of his mercy 'by great and manifest demonstrations'. This was an attempt to split the Jacobite commons from the ruling class and, as such, it was a complete failure. The *Gazette de France* reported on September 2 that the Irish officers were resolved to die fighting rather than accept such harsh terms. The author of *Light to the Blind* observed:

. . . commonly a prince entering into a country in order to conquer it, doth in the first place encourage the principal persons to submit to him, and when these are gained the rest do follow in course. I suppose the Prince of Orange was persuaded to go against reason in favour of his great officers, who would have the Irish Catholic lords of the land to be rejected from all expectation of recovering their estates, because the said officers were sure in their own concerts that the Irish army would be overcome at last, because then they might have those lands by the Prince's grant.

Robert Southwell, who drafted the declaration, explained that it was designed 'to invite in all the meaner sort' but as regards the landed Irish Catholics it was not the policy 'to be meddling with the landed men till it appears into what posture they throw themselves or into what corner they retire'. He felt that by pursuing this policy the declaration would bring in 'the bulk of the nation and the rest will afterwards look the more abject'.

However, the soldiers of William's army did not appreciate the subtleness of politics and killed and pillaged Catholics whether they had asked for protection or not. Story noted that the Ulster colonial regiments 'were very dexterous at that sport.'

On the Tuesday William heard some news from London that dampened his spirits. On June 30 the combined English and Dutch fleets had met the French off Beachy Head and the French had defeated them. In fact, the Cabinet had met and asked Thomas, Marquis of Carmarthen, to write to William to point out the implications of defeat and ask him to return to England. William did not receive Lord Carmarthen's letter until July 16 when he was encamped at Castledermot, Co. Kildare. After congratulating William on 'Drogheda', Lord Carmarthen reported the disaster and pressed William to return. The defeat had created a highly dangerous situation because if England was threatened with an invasion from France, William's return was a matter of urgency. The situation was ripe for a Jacobite uprising in England and Lord Carmarthen urged William either to return, preferably, or to send back part of his army 'so far as it could be done with good manners'. Lord Carmarthen had also heard that the French were now preparing to send twenty-eight frigates into the Irish Sea. William replied that he would send back some troops and that he, himself, would return after six or seven days. He despatched two regiments of foot, a regiment of horse and a dragoon regiment.

On July 9, Würtemberg-Neustadt had written to Jens Harboe that 'King James had abandoned Ireland, so that to all appearences only Limerick can be defended'. The remnants of the Jacobite army, gathered by the Duke of Berwick with the aid of Patrick Sarsfield, had marched across the Liffey on the night of Wednesday, July 2, at Leixlip. They had passed through Chapelizod, on to Naas, through Castledermot, Carlow and Kilkenny and had arrived at Limerick some fifteen days later. According to the author of *Light to the Blind*:

> There followed them a great number of gentlemen, who had no military employment, and of clergy, of farmers and tradesmen, as also of ladies and inferior women and their children, they having an aversion to stay home under the arbiting compartment of an heretical infidel army. The enemy afterwards plundered their houses, took away what cattle they left behind

and seized on their estates and farms. The enemy also committed ('tis a certain truth) some murders in the county of Westmeath and in King's County.

The Jacobite army that collected around Limerick, the colonist's pronunciation of Luimneach, meaning the bare place, comprised about 20,000 infantry and 3,500 cavalry, of which at least one half was not properly armed. The responsibility, as viceroy, fell on Tyrconnell who now had to consider whether he would defend the city or make terms with William. Limerick was an important town, the second city in Ireland with only Dublin exceeding it in size. It had been founded by the Vikings as a settlement in the tenth century. It was well fortified with complete walls, bastions and outworks. Its houses were built of stone 'being made most of them castle ways with battlements'. It stood on the river Shannon which was navigable for ships of large size to come up to the town itself, while smaller craft could come right up to Ballsbridge which connected the two parts of the city known as Englishtown and Irishtown.

Some distance north of the city the Shannon divided into two arms which reunited immediately south of the city, forming a large island two miles in circumference called King's Island. King John built a castle here in 1210. The newer Irishtown spanned the narrow eastern arm of the river, where it bends to the west round the lower end of King's Island. Between the towns stood St. Mary's cathedral, founded by Dónal Mór Ó'Bríen in 1172. It was destroyed by Ireton during the Cromwellian siege but was rebuilt in 1678. King John's Castle stood by Thomond Bridge, just south of it, which connected Englishtown with Co. Clare. The city was therefore in a good strategic position and a good place to defend.

But the Jacobite leaders were now divided. Lauzun observed derisively: 'Why should the English bring cannon against fortifications that could be battered down with roasted apples?' The young Berwick observed that 'the place had no fortifications but all walls without ramparts, and some miserable little towers without ditches. We had made a sort of covered way all round, and a kind of earthwork pallisade before the great gate but the enemy did not attack that side.' The young Duke and the Frenchman were perhaps unnecessarily pessimistic for their accounts do not fit other contemporary descriptions of the fortifications of Limerick.

Colonel O'Kelly backed the energetic Patrick Sarsfield, whom he described as 'the darling of the army', in taking the line that Limerick should be defended. The elderly Tyrconnell, exhausted after the Boyne and in ill-health, was doubtful. Lauzun, writing to Seignelay on July 16, said that Limerick was completely indefensible and that he had no doubt that he and Tyrconnell would soon be prisoners of the Williamites were they to remain there. Several Irishmen were now asking for commissions in the army but Lauzun suspected that they were trying to elevate their rank in order to strike a better bargain with William. A council of war was held and Captain Stevens reported that Tyrconnell had declared that the best course was negotiation with William. He was met with a strong and indignant opposition led by Sarsfield. It was rumoured that the Irish officers would turn the French out of Limerick and defend it on their own. The position was now not one of Louis XIV's allies fighting the Grand Alliance, nor of an attempt to replace James II on the throne of the three kingdoms, but the age old fight of the Irish to repulse the English conqueror. Lauzun wrote to Louvois on July 31 that he was going to withdraw the French regiments to Galway because he did not want them to remain in close quarters with the Irish 'who hate us so much that we fear they will play some dirty trick on us'. He asked that ships be sent to evacuate the French troops and the best of the other Jacobite regiments. He would be 'sorry to see them go to the Prince of Orange, particularly three cavalry regiments which are excellent'.

However, the Jacobite war council finally came to a decision. In spite of the misgivings of Lauzun and Tyrconnell the Jacobites would stand and defend Limerick. Major-General Alexandre Rainier, Marquis de Boisseleau, was to be the military governor of the town. The defending troops would consist of a regiment of cavalry, a regiment of dragoons and twenty-eight infantry regiments making a total of 14,000 men. However, according to Lauzun, many were without arms. Behind Limerick, in Co. Clare, Sarsfield would gather a cavalry force to be used for harrying actions. The Irish Jacobites, in spite of the flight of James, were determined that the shame of the Boyne would be avenged.

'But where is James? What? Urged to fly?'

The news of the victory at the Boyne had reached London on July 7 and was immediately forwarded on to William's allies in the Grand Alliance. The Catholic states of Austria and Spain, long accustomed to Louis' imperial adventures, went into wild rejoicing for the Williamite victory and Te Deum's were sung in Austrian and Spanish cathedrals. A rumour went around that a Te Deum was sung in St. Peter's in Rome and had Pope Innocent XI, the bitter enemy of Louis XIV who had helped finance William's army, still been alive it in all probability would have been. But the new Pope Alexander VIII was less hostile to France than Innocent had been and John Drummond, first earl of Melfort, reported that the new Pope was scandalised by the Te Deums sung in Catholic cathedrals to celebrate the victory. There was great rejoicing throughout all the countries of the Grand Alliance but the defeat of the combined English and Dutch fleets off Beachy Head somewhat marred the celebrations. What *was* the subject of rejoicing, much ridicule and laughter was the flight of James II.

An Ulster colonial song, which soon became popular under the title 'The Boyne Water', pointed out that it was not the Jacobite soldiers who had let James down but James who had let his army down.

> But where is James? What? Urged to fly?
>   'ere quailed his brave defenders!
> Their dead in Oldbridge crowded lie
>   But not a sword surrenders:
> Again they've found the 'vantage ground;
>   Their zeal is still untiring;
> As slowly William hems them round
>   In narrowing ring still firing.

Indeed, where was O'Bruadair's 'noble and steadfast Prince, warlike, illustrious, pious, triumphant and brave to death!' In his poem *Caithrém an dara Seámus*—The Triumph of James—written a few years before, the Cork born poet had heaped praise on James' valour.

> On the lips of our sages and poets is ever
>   That he never kept away from slaughter
> Where his friends were engaged in perilous contests

With superior forces deforming them;
He was often a witness of wounds on a battlefield
Where he acted as cook to the raven
Scion of slaughter, intelligent, serious,
Stirring, aggressive and pillaging.

Of course the praise was not unfounded then, for James did have the attributes of physical courage, sincerity and tenacity. In his youth he had served in the French army under the Maréchal de France Henri de la Tour d'Auvergne, Vicomte de Turenne, who had praised his courage. Louis II de Bourbon, Prince de Condé, has observed that 'in the matter of courage he desired to see nothing better than the Duke of York'. James had also distinguished himself fighting for the Spanish at the Battle of Dunes in 1656. As Lord High Admiral of England in 1665 he had remained on deck for eighteen hours, during a sea battle with the Dutch, exposing himself to such heavy firing that more than one man was killed at his side. Was it then physical cowardice that forced him to flee after the Boyne, when his presence might have easily rallied his army before Dublin? Or, as is more likely, was it simply a disastrous error of judgement?

The Williamite Captain Parker observed that James' flight 'does not answer the character that was given of his behaviour at the battle of the Dunes, and nearer Dunkirk in Flanders, where it was said the Duke of York did wonders'. And Colonel O'Kelly, the Jacobite, pointed out: 'The courage and valour of King James whereof he gave a thousand demonstrations by sea and land, made the world conclude that this flight was not altogether occasioned by an act of pusillanimity, but proceeded rather from a wrong maxim of state.' The author of *Light to the Blind* is more bitter and reflected the majority view of the Irish: '. . . we must conclude that the King had no solid reason to quit Ireland upon the loss he sustained at the Boyne in his troops. For the army was rather somewhat stronger at the end of the petty conflict than before, and at its arrival before Limerick it might have been reinforced by ten thousand resolute men at the least, and might have given battle (as 'twas expected) with the highest probability of victory.'

The Comte d'Avaux had, in fact, prophesied James' flight as far back as October 21, 1689, when he had written to Louis XIV: 'I can assure Your Majesty that he [James] would flee at the first check which would happen to him.' James' allies were bitter at his action. François Henri de Montmorency-Bouteville, Duc de Luxembourg, fresh from his victory over the Williamite commander Prince Georg Friedrich of Waldeck, commented scathingly: 'Those who love the King of England must be very glad to see him safe and sound, but those who think of his reputation have reason to deplore the figure he has cut.' The Marquis de Louvois was even angrier and said James had 'spoiled everything by a mixture of ignorance, over confidence and folly'.

The Williamites celebrated by striking a medal which portrayed James running away after the Boyne and, on the reverse side, was a deer with winged hooves and the Latin inscription 'pedibus timor addidit alas'. And soon a new play was playing to packed theatres in London called *The Royal Flight*, a farce in which James was depicted as a petulant coward and in which, significantly enough, Patrick Sarsfield emerged as an Irish hero.

In later life James admitted he had made 'a wrong resolution'. He blamed his generals and his privy councillors and said it was their fault for advising him to leave. They had, he said: 'rashly . . . advised such disheartening councils as to make His Majesty seem to abandon a cause which had still so much hope of life in it. He had all the best parts [of the country] and some of the strongest places behind him, he had leisure enough to see if the army, which was very little diminished by the action, might not have rallied again, which his presence would hugely have contributed to, and his speedy flight must needs discourage from. He might be sure his own people, and especially the court of France, would be hardly induced to maintain a war which he himself had so hastily abandoned.'

'But, on the other hand', he went on, in justification, 'it was not so much wondered that the King should be prevailed upon to do it, considering the unanimous advice of his council, of the generals themselves and all persons about him.' The only two generals who gave such advice were, of course, Lauzun and Tyrconnell, of whom James says: 'it is wondered on what grounds my lord Tyrconnell thought fit to press it with so much earnestness, unless it was out of a tenderness to the Queen'. James tried to describe the panic of those around him, urging him to fly, especially that of the four French officers, de la Hoguette, Chemérault, Mérode and Famechon. He refers to 'that universal panic and fear which could make those French officers (men of service) see visions of troops when none could certainly be within twenty miles of them'. This, he said, 'excused in great measure the King taking so wrong a resolution'. But, and significantly, James claims: 'All that would not have determined him to leave Ireland so soon had he not conceived it the likeliest expedient to repair his losses accordingly to a certain scheme he had formed to himself, and which in reality had been laid by the court of France.' The scheme was for James to leave William tied up in Ireland while he went to France, raised an army, and with the defeat of the Anglo–Dutch fleets at Beachy Head and the sea routes open, invade England. However, James could not have known of the defeat of the Anglo–Dutch fleets until after he had returned to France. It is true that James tried to press the plan on Louis on his return but the French, having seen how James led his armies, rejected the idea out of hand. Whether the scheme had been thought up by James on his journey to France to justify his flight, or whether he had genuinely thought of the invasion idea when he reached Dublin after the battle (although he would not at that time have been able to count on the open sea routes), the timing of the plan was ridiculous and showed James' complete lack of understanding of how his fellow men would regard his action.

Only his loyal son, the Duke of Berwick, accepted his father's account of the flight without question.

The King seeing from the ill success of the battle of the Boyne that he could not keep possession of Dublin, thought it better to leave the command to Tyrconnell and return to France, as well to solicit a reinforcement as to see if he could not find an opening to take advantage of the absence of the Prince of Orange for an attempt upon England. The opportunity was favourable, for Marshal Luxembourg gained the battle of Fleurus in Flanders and the Comte de Tourville, who had lately beaten the enemy's fleet, was then at anchor in the Downs, so that passage to England being without difficulty or opposition, it was presumed that the King might with ease make himself master of the kingdom.

This would likewise oblige the Prince of Orange to quit Ireland in order to save the greater stake, but M. de Louvois, Minister for the War Department, thwarted all the projects of the King of England and set himself so strongly to counteract the plan that the Most Christian King [Louis XIV] overcome by his arguments, refused to consent to it.

To 'save face' James put the blame for the loss of the battle on the Irish troops, and in this he was supported by the French generals who wished to exonerate themselves. These false stories were believed by the French populace. Colonel O'Kelly recorded: 'The Irish merchants who lived there [Paris] since the conquest of Oliver Cromwell durst not walk abroad, nor appear in the streets, the people were so exasperated against them.' No Irishman was safe on the streets for many weeks. Only Colonel Conrad Zurlauben, whose account was never officially published, laid the blame in the right place. Basically, William had been the better general. James had fallen for his feint and moved the bulk of his army away from the main battle zone, leaving a small force to face the main body of the Williamites and, without reinforcements, it was inevitable they would be overcome. But James preferred to lay the blame elsewhere. His distaste of the Irish showed clearly when, two years later, he wrote some instructions to his son telling him that the main garrisons in Ireland must never be entrusted to Irish governors or Irish troops. The sons of the principal families in Ireland must be given an English education so that they could be 'weaned away from their natural hatred against the English'. Schools should be set up in Ireland that would teach English, and 'by degrees wear out the Irish language, which would be for the advantage of the inhabitants'. No native of Ireland should be a lord-lieutenant and the native Irish who lost their estates from the time of James I were to be told that they had no hope of being restored to those estates under any English monarch.

James' hatred of the Irish was returned in kind by the Irish themselves. The flight of the Stuart monarch after the Boyne only completed an alienation that began as soon as the Irish people realised that James had no sympathy with the national aspirations of Ireland and that he looked upon the country as no more than a convenient stepping stone to recover England. To the Irish James became *Séamus an Chaca*, James the Shithead. Lord Clare, writing to Louvois on August 22, 1690, felt that James would do better to spend the rest of his days praying in a cloister rather than trying to command armies or govern a state. The Stuart cause in Ireland died after the battle of the Boyne, although the struggle against William continued for another eighteen months. To the Irish, however, it was no longer a war for the Stuarts. The motives were different and the views of the leaders were different. It had become a war to drive out the English led by such Irish officers as Patrick Sarsfield. The monarchy was irrelevant. Indeed, Bishop Burnet put a phrase into Sarsfield's mouth which summed up the Irish attitude: 'As low as we now are, change but Kings with us and we will fight it over again with you.'

In the succeeding months after James' flight the Irish proved that they could fight indeed. Although the Williamite James Douglas took Athlone with comparative ease a few days after the battle at the Boyne, the Jacobite stand at Limerick was no easy contest. William did not arrive before Limerick until August 8, by which time Bentinck had driven in the Irish outposts, and called upon the town to surrender. By the end of August the Williamites were still trying to storm the walls. The safety of the city was attributed to a dashing attack made by Sarsfield with a small force of 400 horse and 200 dragoon. After a spectacular night ride, Sarsfield intercepted William's artillery and siege train at Ballyneety and destroyed it, leaving the Williamite army with practically no artillery with which to storm the city. On August 29 William gave the order to retreat. Within a few days he had returned to London leaving the conduct of the war in the hands of his Dutch general Godard van Reede, Baron Ginkel, whom he created first Earl of Athlone. The Jacobite commanders Tyrconnell and Lauzun left Ireland for France at the same time, leaving the Duke of Berwick in command.

And so the war dragged on. John Churchill, Duke of Marlborough, arrived in September and his successful siege of Cork and Kinsale did not dampen Jacobite enthusiasm. The winter skirmishes and attempted negotiations only sharpened the Jacobite appetite for a decisive conflict. Tyrconnell returned and with him a new French commander. The arrival on May 9 of Charles Chalmont, Marquis de St. Ruth, was greeted with jubilation by the Jacobites. Here, at last, was a seasoned field commander. To the Williamites the arrival of St. Ruth was 'like pouring brandy down a dying man's throat'. But St. Ruth's first action at Athlone in June was a defeat for the Jacobite army. Then, on July 12, came the singular disaster of Aughrim. The Jacobites had the advantage, victory was in sight, when St. Ruth was killed by artillery. Muddled orders and panic created general disorder and the Jacobite army began to flee. For the Irish nation it was, perhaps, their most disastrous battle.

Some 7,000 were reported killed with 400 officers, most of them scions of Irish nobility and Old English nobility. Colonel O'Kelly observed that on that day the Irish lost 'the flower of their army and nation'.

By the end of July Galway had fallen and the Jacobite army fell back on Limerick. On August 14 Tyrconnell had a stroke and died and James, blundering once again, turned over the administration to his English advisers. The Irish seemed to lose heart and by August 25 Ginkel was attacking Limerick. The Jacobites still contested the city but on September 23 the Irish and French generals held a meeting and decided resistance was useless. Negotiations were opened at which Patrick Sarsfield played a prominent part and by October 3 a draft treaty was signed.

The French were allowed to return home and those Irish Jacobites who surrendered were allowed to return to their homes unmolested or to take service abroad, as their fathers had done in Cromwell's time. More importantly, a promise of religious freedom was given and also a pledge that not all the estates of the Jacobite adherents would be confiscated. For the majority of the Irish the concession of religious liberty was welcomed enthusiastically. The Williamites promised that the Catholic population would be granted 'not less toleration' than they enjoyed prior to James II's accession. The Treaty was adhered to insofar as 12,000 Irish soldiers, led by Sarsfield, left to go into exile in the service of France, Spain and Austria. So began another great Irish diaspora—the fabled 'flight of the wild geese' who were to form the famous fighting Irish brigades in the armies of France and Spain. A diaspora which gave birth to such men as Marshal Patrick MacMahon, Duke of Magenta, president of the French Republic from 1873–79; Marshal Leopold O'Donnell, Duke of Tetuan, prime minister of Spain from 1860–68 and Viscount Taafe of Roscommon, Imperial Chancellor of the Austro–Hungarian Empire, and many others. Ireland's loss seemed Europe's gain.

Sarsfield, who negotiated the treaty, led his troops into the service of Louis XIV and was one of the first to die in the subsequent War of the Grand Alliance which kept William and Louis at each other's throats from 1693–97. Sarsfield fell during an engagement at Landen, in Holland, during the great battle of Neerwinden in which defeat William lost 18,000 men. As Sarsfield fell dying he is reported to have said 'if only it was for Ireland'.

And the Treaty of Limerick? The Williamites failed to ratify it. Some 1,500,000 acres were confiscated for a new colonisation scheme. The religious freedom became a myth. The Jacobite Parliament, sitting in Dublin in 1689, had tried to abolish all religious discrimination by law, passing Acts XIII and XV; they declared that all religions should be equal under the law and that each priest or minister should be supported by his own congregation only, and that no tithes should be levied upon any person for the support of a church to which he did not belong. But after William's victory the only religion recognised was that of the Church of England. Penal laws were enacted against Catholic and dissenting Protestant.

In William's 'new era of religious freedom' a Presbyterian minister was liable to three months in jail for delivering a sermon and a fine of £100 for celebrating the Lord's Supper. Presbyterians were punished if they were discovered to have been married by a Presbyterian minister. An Act in 1704 excluded all Presbyterians from holding office in the law, army, navy, customs and excise or municipal employment. In 1715 a further act made it an offence for Presbyterian ministers to teach children and this was punishable with three months in prison. Intermarriage between Presbyterians and Anglicans was declared illegal. As late as 1772 Presbyterians were punished for holding religious meetings.

The 'religious liberty' won by William of Orange in 1691 caused some 250,000 Protestant Ulstermen to migrate to America between the years 1717 and 1776 alone in order to find religious liberty. It was the descendants of these Presbyterian Ulstermen, so called 'Scotch-Irish', who were to play a prominent part in the American War of Independence and the creed of republicanism was to find a fertile ground among them and their cousins still in Ireland. Soon after, it was this republican philosophy that united the Protestant and Catholic, who had suffered similarly after William's victory, under the common name of Irishmen in their bid to throw out the English imperial yoke. The administration was aware of the danger as Hugh Boulter, Anglican Archbishop of Armagh, wrote at the time:

The worst of this is that it stands to unite Protestant and Papist and whenever that happens, goodbye to the English interest in Ireland forever.

It was from that time that all Protestants in Ireland were singled out for 'special treatment', and the Boyne became symbolic of the distortion of Irish history. For modern day Irish sectarianism did not begin at the Boyne, it began with the defeat of the Protestant and Catholic Irish uprising of 1798. Then what of the Boyne? It was, from both the Williamite and Jacobite viewpoint, where the Stuart monarchy in the British Isles was overthrown. The Irish had been misled into supporting the Stuarts, equating the Stuart cause with the restoration of their land and national dignity. An Irish poet has summed it up:

> *Se tigheacht Righ Seamas do chain dinn Éire*
> It is the coming of King James that took Ireland from us,
> With his one shoe English and his one shoe Irish.
> He would neither strike a blow, nor would he come to terms
> And that has left, so long as they shall exist,
>   misfortune upon the Irish.

SOURCES AND
ACKNOWLEDGEMENTS

In my account of the Cromwellian colonisation of Ireland, *Hell or Connaught!* (Hamish Hamilton, 1975) I dispensed with the system of using copious footnotes for source references because I did not wish to claim academic status for the work to which I did not feel it was entitled as I was not, in fact, setting out to write an academic work. Similarly, with this volume I am writing a reconstruction of the battle aimed essentially for the non-academic. For those who wish to research more on the subject this selected bibliography names my principal sources and is divided up into 'eye-witness accounts' and general works. At the time of writing Professor John Gerald Simms' outstanding work *Jacobite Ireland 1685–91* (Routledge and Kegan Paul, London, 1969) must remain the premier study on the period and the principal source book for all students.

For helping me research for illustrations for this work I want to make a special thanks to Miss May Boyd of the photographic section of Board Fáilte Éireann for the photographs of the battle site today.

BIBLIOGRAPHY

Eye Witness Accounts

A composite introduction to these accounts may be found in 'Eye Witnesses to the Boyne' by J. G. Simms, *Irish Sword*, Vol. VI, Summer, 1963, No. 22.

Danish accounts can be found in the National Library of Ireland, micro film regs. 1026, 3216 and 3253.

French accounts can be found in the Bibliothèque Nationale, Paris, under Ministère de la guerre, archives anciennes, Vols 960/962.

A true relation of the battle of the Boyne in Ireland, April 11, 1690.

An Account of King William's royal heading of the men of Inniskillin, London, 1690.

Two Unpublished Diaries Connected with the battle of the Boyne, Ulster Journal of Archaeology, Belfast, Vol. IV (first series) 1853.

BELLINGHAM, Sir Thomas, Diary, ed. Anthony Hewitson, Preston, 1908.

BENTINCK, Hans Willem (aft. Duke of Portland) author of official account for William, Narrative of the fight at the Boyne—Royal Irish Academy Ms 24 G i No 38. See also letter to Earl of Melville dated July 4, Melville and Leven Papers, pp. 459–62.

BERWICK, Duke of (James Fitzjames) Memoirs. 2 vols, London 1779.

BONNIVERT, Gideon, Journal. See Journal of Louth Archaeological Society, Vol VIII pages 18–27, Dundalk and Drogheda, 1904.

BOSTAQUET, Dumont de. Mémoires Inédits. p. 272.

BREWER, Richard, letter to Thomas Wharton, Carte MSS 79, Bodleian Library, Oxford.

CLARKE, George, Autobiography, see Leyborne-Popham MSS, publication of the Historical Manuscripts Commission, 1899.

CLAUDIANUS, Andreas. Mavors Irlandicus, sive historia de bello Hibernico biennium in Hibernia gesto, chartis consignata a commilitone. A.C. Copenhagen, 1718. (Irish Mars, or a history of the war waged in Ireland for two years from notes recorded by a fellow soldier AC). See also Studies, J. Jordan, vol. XLIII pp. 431/2.

DAVIES, Rowland. Journal of the Very Reverend Rowland Davies LL.D. (Dean of Ross, aft. Dean of Cork) from March 8, 1688–9 to September 29, 1690, edited by Richard Caulfield, Camden Society, London, 1857.

DOUGLAS, Lt. General James, letter to Duke of Queensberry dated July 7, 1690. M. Napier vol. III p. 715.

FOULERESSE, Jean Payen de la, Danish ambassador. Letter dated Duleek, July 2, 1690. Notes and Queries, 5th series, Vol. VIII, July 14, 1877.

HOP, Jacob, Dutch envoy extraordinary to States-General of Holland, account dated July 2, 1690. Europische Mercurius, July, 1690, pp. 64/5.

HOGUETTE, Marquis de la. Letters to Louvois from Kinsale, July 4, 1690 and July 31, 1690. Min. Guerre. 961 nos. 152, 176.

LAUZUN, Comte de. Letters to Seignelay, July 16, 1690. Reprinted in Von Ranke's History of England.

MEATH, Lord. Letter dated July 5, 1690. See Royal Irish Academy, Reg. Proc. IX, 534–5.

MULLENAUX, Samuel MD. A Journal of the three month royal campaign of His Majesty in Ireland. London, 1690.

PARKER, Robert. Memoirs of Captain Robert Parker, late of the Royal Regiment of Foot, published by his son at Dame Street, Dublin. 1747.

SOUTHWELL, Sir Robert. Letter to Lord Nottingham dated July 1/2, 1690. Historical Manuscripts Commission, Finch MSS II, 326–9.

ST. FELIX. Aide to Count Schomberg. Letter to Countess Schomberg dated July 2, 1690. See J. F. A. Kazner's Leben Friedrichs von Schomberg oder Schoenberg, Mannheim, 1789, 2 vols. (In vol. II, pp. 353–8.)

STEVENS, John. The Journal of John Stevens, ed. Robert H. Murray, Clarendon Press, Oxford, 1912.

STORY, George Warter. A True and impartial history of the most material occurences in the kingdom of Ireland during the last two years, London, 1691.

VILLARE HIBERNICUM, or a view of His Majesty's Conquest in Ireland during his presence there, printed by W. Griffiths Esq. London, 1690.

General works

Calendar of State Papers, May 1690–October 1691, edited by William John Hardy, HMSO, 1898.

Journal of the House of Commons of the Kingdom of Ireland, May 18, 1613—August 2, 1800. Dublin, 1796–1800.

Abridgement of the English Military Discipline printed by His Majesty's special command for the use of His Majesty's forces. London, 1686.

A Full Account of King William's Royal Voyage and safe arrival at the castle of Belfast. London. 1690.

BAGWELL, Richard. Ireland Under the Stuarts and during the Interregnum, 3 vols. Longmans Green, London, 1909.

BAXTER, Stephen. William III, Longmans, London, 1966.

BOULGER, D. C. The Battle of the Boyne. Martin Secker, London, 1911.

BURNET, Gilbert, History of His Own Times, 6 vols. Clarendon Press, Oxford, 1823.

BRUNE, Jean de la. Histoire de la Revolution d'Irland arrive sous Guillaume III, Amsterdam, 1791.

D'ALTON, J. King James' Irish Army List 1689, Dublin, 1890.

DANAHER, Kevin and SIMMS, J. G. The Danish Force in Ireland 1690–1. Dublin. 1962.

GILBERT, John Thomas, ed. A Jacobite Narrative of the War in Ireland 1688–91 (originally entitled A Light to the Blind whereby they may see the dethronement of James the Second, King of England, with a brief narrative of his war in Ireland, and of the war between the emperor and king of France for the crown of Spain. Anno 1711—ascribed to Nicholas Plunkett, a lawyer). Dublin, 1892.

LUCAS, Etienne. Imago Regis. Paris, 1693.

MACCARTNEY-Filgate, E. The War of William III in Ireland, Longmans London 1906.

MURRAY, Robert H. Revolutionary Ireland and its Settlement, Macmillan, London, 1911.

O'KELLY, Charles. Macariae Excidium or the Destruction of Cyprus, Camden Society, London 1841. Then edited by Count G. N. Plunkett as The Jacobite War in Ireland 1688–1691, Dubin, 1894.

PETRIE, Sir Charles. The Marshal Duke of Berwick, Eyre and Spottiswoode, London, 1953.

SERGEANT, P. W. Little Jennings and Fighting Dick Talbot, 2 vols. London, 1913.

SIMMS, John Gerald. Jacobite Ireland 1685–91, Routledge and Kegan Paul, London, 1969.

SIMMS, John Gerald. The Williamite Confiscation in Ireland 1690–1703. Faber and Faber, London, 1956.

   (See also under DANAHER, Kevin, and section Eye Witnesses.)

VON RANKE, Leopold. A History of England, Clarendon Press, Oxford, 1875.

WILDE, William. Beauties of the Boyne, McGlashen, Dublin, 1849.

WITHEROW, Thomas. The Boyne and Aughrim, William Mullen, Belfast, 1879.

INDEX

Account of King William's royal heading of the men of Inniskillin, An, 108

Alexander VIII, Pope, 144

Anne, Princess (later Queen), 8, 16, 21, 22

Antrim, Alexander MacDonnell, 3rd Earl of, 88; regiment of, 13, 87, 88, 91, 94

Ardee, 19, 27, 40, 41, 42, 48–9, 50–2, 53, 54

Argyle, Archibald Campbell, 9th Earl of, 6

Arklow, 128

Armagh, 46, 47

Art of Shooting Great Ordnance, The (Bourne), 26

Ashton, Major Arthur, 90

Athlone, 149

Athy, 136, 137

Aughrim, 31, 149–50

Auverquerque, Count Henry Nassau, Lord, 22, 69, 90–1, 94, 135, 137

Avaux, Jean-Antoine de Mesmes, Comte d', 18, 86, 145

Belasye, Sir Henry, 48

Belfast, 19, 22–5, 32–3

Belfast Lough, 15, 17, 22

Bellingham, Colonel Sir Thomas, 1, 23–4, 25, 38, 39, 50, 53, 57, 61, 62, 84, 88, 97, 119, 121, 130, 132, 135, 136, 137, 138

Bellow, Lord John, 32

Belturbet, 46

Bentinck, Hans Willem (later Earl of Portland), 21, 43, 64, 66, 69, 103, 104, 116, 133, 149

Berwick, James Fitzjames, Duke of, 5, 18, 28, 36, 39, 58, 63, 65, 70, 85, 86, 91, 92, 95, 96, 98, 106, 110, 112, 117–19, 124, 141, 142, 147, 149

Billington, William, 139

Biron, Colonel, regiment of, 30, 80

Blackhall, George, 139

Blaris Moor, 35

Bloody Bridge, 125

Boisseleau, Alexandre Rainier, Marquis de, 82, 143

Bonnivert, Gideon, 32, 47–8, 49, 52, 60–1, 77, 79, 119, 136

Bostaquet, Dumont de, 103, 105, 107, 109

Bouilly, Colonel, regiment of, 30, 80

Boulter, Hugh, Anglican archbishop of Armagh, 151

Bourne, William, 26

'Boyne Water, The' (song), 144

Braddock, John, 139

Brasil, 123

Bray, 128, 129

Brewer, Richard, 82

Brewerton, Captain, 106

Browne, Nicholas, regiment of, 81

Bulmer, René, 34

Bunyan, John, 7

Burnet, Bishop Gilbert, 21, 22, 69, 72, 115–16, 120, 149

Caillimote, Colonel, 43, 95; regiment of, 90, 94, 95, 96

Caithréim Theidhg (Ó Bruadair), 13, 144

Cambron, Colonel, 43; regiment of, 46, 90, 94, 96

Carlingford, Francis, 3rd Earl of, 92

Carmarthen, Marquis of—*see* Danby, Thomas Osborne, Earl of

Carney, Sir Charles, 81

Carrickfergus Castle, 17

Carroll, Francis, regiment of, 111

Castle Caulfield, 102

Castleblaney, 46

Castledermot, 141

Castletown Bellow, 29, 31–2, 41, 50

Castleton, Philip, 139

Cavendish, Lord, regiment of, 25, 32, 47, 50, 56, 76, 139

Charles II, 6, 10

Chémerault, Colonel, 117, 124, 129, 146; regiment of, 30, 80

Clanricarde, John de Burgh, 9th Earl of, regiment of, 87, 88

Clare, Daniel O'Brien, 3rd Viscount, 148; regiment of, 86, 104–5, 106

Clarendon, Henry Hyde, 2nd Earl of, 9, 11, 31, 85

Clarke, George, 22, 46–7, 70, 83–4, 91, 92, 103, 120

Claudinus, Andreas, 97

Clifford, Robert, regiment of, 111

Collins, Sir Grenville, 16

Compton, Henry, bishop of London, 8

Condé, Louis II de Bourbon, Prince de, 145

Coningsby, Thomas, 24, 64, 68

Cork, 149

Creagh, Sir Michael, regiment of, 138

Cross, Captain Haws, 56

Cunningham, Sir Albert, regiment of, 43, 102

Cutts, Colonel John, regiment of, 93, 97

Dalrymple, Sir John, 114

Danby, Thomas Osborne, Earl of (later Marquis of Carmarthen), 8, 9, 120, 141

Davies, Captain Rowland, 24, 25, 32, 35, 38, 39, 47, 50, 52, 54, 56, 76, 77, 82, 120, 130, 133, 135, 137, 138–9

Declaration of Indulgence (1687), 7

Declaration of Rights (1689), 9

Dempsey, Lieutenant-Colonel Laurence, 37, 38

Derry, 16, 34; regiments from, 17, 35, 90

Desmynieres, John, 139

Devonshire, William Cavendish, 1st Duke of, 8

Dongan, Lord Walter, 104, 114; regiment of, 86, 102, 103–4, 106, 118

Donop, Colonel Montz Melchior von, regiment of, 40, 109

Donore, 59, 62, 81; hill of, 59, 60, 81, 85, 91, 107, 108–9

Dopping, Anthony, Anglican bishop of Meath, 34, 134, 139

Dorrington, Major-General William, 87, 88, 106, 107

Douglas, Lieutenant-General James, 25, 35, 39, 42, 64, 68, 69, 80, 81, 82, 84, 97, 104, 112, 115, 149

Dover, Henry Jermyn, Viscount, 86

Dover, Treaty of (1670), 6–7

Dowth tumulus, 59, 77

Drogheda, Lord, regiment of, 43, 54–5

Drogheda, 18, 51, 53, 54, 57, 58, 59–61, 85, 130–1, 141

Drybridge, 83, 103, 106

Dublin, 5, 14, 16, 28–9, 33–4, 54, 57, 72, 122–8, 132, 134–40

Duleek, 69, 74, 83, 107, 110, 112–13, 114, 115, 116, 117, 119, 130, 135

Duncannon, 129–30

Dundalk, 18, 19, 29, 31, 32, 34, 35, 36, 39, 40, 41, 46, 47, 48, 49, 50, 51, 55, 57

Enniscorthy, 129

Enniskillen, 16, 26; regiments from, 17, 20, 22, 35–6, 49, 68, 87, 90, 94, 98, 99, 104, 107–8, 109

Eppinger, Colonel, regiment of, 43, 51, 77, 79

Famechon, Colonel, 117, 124, 129, 146

Farlow, Captain, 37, 38, 47, 128, 134

Finglas, 42, 138, 139

Fitzgerald, Lieutenant-Colonel, 38

Fitzgerald, Captain Robert, 128, 134–5

Fitzjames, Henry, Lord Grand Prior of England, 124; regiment of, 30–2, 41, 46, 81, 92, 113–14, 118, 119, 126, 127, 138

Foley, Samuel, 34

Forest-Suzannet, Frédéric Henri, Marquis de la, 95

Fouleresse, Jean Payen de la (Danish ambassador), 54, 60, 64, 69, 88, 89, 90, 91, 93, 96, 99, 102, 104, 109, 110, 115, 117, 120, 121, 131, 132–3

Franklin, Sir William, 22

Full Account of King William's Royal Voyage, A, 23

Galmoy, Pierce Butler, 3rd Viscount, 36, 96; regiment of, 30, 32, 95

Galway, 71, 150

Gam, Lieutenant-Colonel Karl Gustav von, 53–4

Gazette de France, 140

Georg of Daamstadt, Prince, 16, 21–2, 35, 39, 57, 63, 84

Gillestown bog, 82

Ginkel, Godet de, 22, 102, 103, 106–7, 133, 149, 150; regiment of, 43, 105, 106–7

Golborne, Dan, 35

Gore, Sir Robert, 134

Gosworth, Lord, 123

Grand Prior—*see* Fitzjames, Henry

Gravemoor, Heer van 's, 40, 41, 42, 47, 57, 60

Great news from the army (news-sheet), 17

Grove Island, 58, 63, 89, 90, 91, 103

Gustavus II Adolphus of Sweden, 25

Gwynn, Colonel, regiment of, 43

Hamilton, Major-General Anthony, 82, 110

Hamilton, Gustavus, 22, 87; Enniskillen troops, 35, 43, 68, 90, 94

Hamilton, Major-General John, 82, 110

Hamilton, Lieutenant-General Richard, 72–3, 87, 91, 94, 107, 108–10

Hamilton, William, 13

Hanmer, Colonel Sir John, regiment of, 90, 94–5

Hansen, Wichman, 40

Harboe, Jens, 40, 41, 48, 133, 141

Herbert, Admiral Arthur, 16

Hill, Sir Arthur, 48

Hillsborough, 35, 47–8

Hoguette, Marquis de la, 37, 73, 80–1, 111, 112–13, 116, 117, 124, 129, 130, 146

Hop, Jacob, 119, 133

Hoquincourt, Marquis d', 87, 106

Howard, Hugh, 128

Hoylake, 15, 17

Huygens, Constantijn, 22

Innocent XI, Pope, 9–10, 144

Iveagh, Brian Magennis, 5th Viscount, 59, 131; regiment of, 67, 130

James II: his army, 4, 29–30, 47; decision to fight at Boyne, 4–5, 35, 57–8, 70–5; events leading to deposition, 5–8; regards Ireland as means of regaining throne, 10, 13–14, 15, 148; enters Dublin, 14–15; leaves Dublin to join army at Ardee, 27–8, 29, 39, 48–9; decides to fight for Dublin, 29, 54; rejects advice to retreat, 37; resolves to give up Dundalk, 39, 48, 71; choice of battleground at Boyne, 57–9; personal courage, 70, 145; stubbornness in defending Boyne position, 70–5; deceived by William's strategy, 74–5, 80–2, 110–11; hears of enemy crossing of river, 83, 110; Lauzun's advice to, 112–13, 123, 146; retreats to Dublin, 113–21; William's concern for, 115–16; alleged plan to flee before battle, 119–20; enters Dublin, 123–4, 132; decides to leave for France, 123, 124, 125,

132; flight, 128–30, 133, 144–9; leaves Ireland, 130; losses, 132; apportionment of blame, 145–9
James, Prince of Wales, 8, 86
Jervis, Sir Humphrey, 139
Johnson, Richard, 128

Kalneyn, Colonel Wulff Heinrich, 40
Kilcullen, 127, 136
Kilkenny, 137–8
Kilmainham, 126
Kilmallock, Dominic Sarsfield, 5th Viscount, 126
King, William, dean of St. Patrick's, Dublin, 13, 34, 134, 138
King William's Glen, 62, 63
Kinsale, 14, 85, 130, 149
Kirk, Major-General Percy, 16, 25, 36, 41, 42, 46, 50, 68, 84, 86, 107
Knowth tumulus, 59, 77
Knox, Captain Thomas, 137

La Mellonière, Brigadier de, 43, 130–1; division of, 93, 97
Lanier, Sir John, 22, 56–7; regiment of, 56, 57
Lauzun, Antonin de Caumont, Comte de, 4, 5, 28, 29, 37, 57, 63, 71, 72, 73, 80, 81, 82, 111, 112–13, 116, 117, 123, 124, 125, 129, 142–3, 146, 149
Legacory, 55
Leixlip, 124, 125, 141
Lery de Girardin, Marquis, 29, 72, 79, 80, 82, 111
Levison, Colonel, 110; regiment of, 43, 102, 106
Light to the Blind (attrib. Plunkett), 38, 73–4, 132, 133, 140, 141, 145
Lillebulero, 12, 85, 89
Limerick, 125, 141–3, 145, 149, 150; Treaty of (1691), 150, 151
Lisburn, Lord, 43, 82
Lisburn, 19, 33, 34–5, 47
Lloyd, Thomas, 36
London Gazette, 16, 17, 19, 138
Longford, Francis Aungier, 1st Earl of, 139

Loughbrickland, 39, 47, 48
Louis XIV of France, 4, 6, 7, 8, 9–10, 14, 15, 37, 144, 147
Louth, 31, 48
Louvois, Marquis de, 29, 71, 146, 147
Lucar, Cyprian, 26–7
Luttrell, Henry, 28; regiment of, 51
Luttrell, Narcissus, 132
Luttrell, Simon, 28, 33, 122, 127; regiment of, 28, 124, 126
Luxembourg, Marshal Duc de, 70, 123, 146, 147

Macarie Excidium, or the Destruction of Cyprus (O'Kelly), 72
MacCarthy, Dermot, 12
MacDermott, Terence, 124, 138
Macedon Point, 22
MacGillicuddy, Colonel Denis, 28, 33, 122, 127
MacMahon, Marshal Patrick (Duke of Magenta), 150
Manchester, Charles Montagu, 1st Duke of, 21, 68
Marlborough, John Churchill, 1st Duke of, 6, 8, 92, 149
Marsh, Francis, archbishop of Dublin, 34
Mary, Queen, 7, 8, 9, 69
Mary of Modena, Queen, 8, 9, 29, 72, 123, 133
Matthews, Colonel, 39, 43
Maxwell, Major-General Thomas, 17, 82, 111, 112, 123
Meath, Lord, 82; regiment of, 43, 49
Mee, Giles, 139
Melfort, John Drummond, 1st Earl of, 144
Mellifont Abbey, 3, 61, 66
Mérode, Colonel, 117, 124, 129, 146
Mitchell, Michael, 139
Molley, Walter, 139
Monknewtown, 76, 77
Monmouth, Duke of, 6
Mountcashel, Justin MacCarthy, Viscount, 28

Mountjoy, William Stewart, 1st Viscount, 110

Moyry Pass, 5, 18, 38–9, 46, 47, 50, 128

Mullenaux, Samuel, 23, 35, 53, 99

Mulloy family, 105

Naas, 126, 127, 141

Nagle, Sir Richard, 123

Nantes, Edict of, revocation of (1686), 7, 9, 16

Narrative of the Fight at the Boyne (Bentinck), 133

Nassau, Count Henry—*see* Auverquerque, Lord

Naul, 118, 119

Navan, 35, 74

Newgrange tumulus, 59, 77–8

Newry, 18, 35, 41, 48, 49

Newtownbutler, 16, 34

Nottingham, Daniel Finch, 2nd Earl of, 133

Nottingham, 8

Nova Sciento Invento, La (Tartaglia), 26

O'Brien, John, 65

Ó Bruadair, Daithi, 13, 144

O'Donnell, Marshal Leopold (Duke of Tetuan), 150

O'Donnell, Lieutenant-Colonel, 127

O'Gara, Oliver, regiment of, 96, 105

O'Keefe, John, 65

O'Kelly, Colonel Charles, 11, 30, 71–2, 73, 81, 87, 115, 118, 143, 145, 148, 150

O'Neill, Cormac, 17

O'Neill, Sir Neil, 73, 79–80

O'Toole, Sir Cathal, 99

Oldbridge, 1–3, 53, 58, 59, 60, 62–3, 67–9, 70, 74–5, 80–1, 83–91, 94, 97, 98, 102, 103, 104–7, 110, 112, 114, 115, 117, 119, 121

Ormonde, James Butler, 1st Duke of, 11

Ormonde, James Butler, 2nd Duke of, 21, 35, 39, 135, 137

Oxford, Aubrey de Vere, 20th Earl of, 42, 46, 68

Parker, Colonel John, 63, 98; regiment of, 86, 91, 98, 106

Parker, Captain Robert, 131–2, 145

Perkins, Anthony, 139

'Person of Quality, A', memoir by, 27, 28–9, 33, 54, 122, 125, 127, 128, 132, 135

Platen Castle, 109, 110

Plunkett, Nicholas, 73

Plunkett, Archbishop Oliver, 11

Powis, William Herbert, Duke of, 123, 124

Pownel, Captain, 60, 67, 68, 77

Poynings' Law, 14, 15

Prepetit, Isaac de, 80

Present State of Europe, The (anon.), 65

Purcell, Daniel, 12

Purcell, Nicholas, regiment of, 81, 123

Randall, Francis, 129

Ransford, Mark, 139

Rawdon, Sir Arthur, 35, 39

Rosen, Marshal Conrad von, 18, 36

Rosnaree, 67, 68, 69, 75, 77, 78–80, 81, 82, 83, 84, 123

Royal Flight, The (play), 146

St. Felix (aide to Count Schomberg), 76, 79, 80, 84, 88

St. Germain, 9, 14

St. John, Colonel, regiment of, 90

St. Ruth, Charles Chalmont, Marquis de, 149

Sancroft, Archbishop, 7

Sanders, William, 133

Sanderson, Captain, 16

Sarsfield, Major-General Patrick, 5, 36, 51, 58, 63, 82, 111–12, 128, 141, 143, 146, 149, 150; regiment of, 30, 113, 122

Scarborough, Richard Lumley, Earl of, 8, 21, 68

Schomberg, Friedrich Herman, Duke of, 16–20, 22, 25, 28, 32, 33, 34, 35, 39, 42, 43, 46, 47, 57, 64, 67–8, 70, 93, 95, 98–9, 102–3, 117, 120

Schomberg, Meinhard, Count, 22, 43, 68–9, 76–80, 82, 84, 88, 104, 111, 112, 113, 114–15, 120

Shales, John, 17

Shanganagh, 137

Sheldon, Lieutenant-General Dominic, 47, 87, 92, 94, 106, 107

Shewing the Properties, Office and Duties of a Gunner (Lucar), 26–7

Shovell, Sir Cloudesley, 16, 49

Shrewsbury, Charles Talbot, 12th Earl of, 8

Sidney, Henry, 8, 21, 57, 68, 107

Slane, 58, 60, 67, 68, 69, 72, 74–5, 76, 77, 79, 81, 82

Slaughter, Captain, 134

Smith, John (Dublin alderman), 139

Solms-Braunfels, Heinrich, Count of, 22, 42, 43, 46, 50, 57, 68, 89–90

Southwell, Sir Robert, 22, 84, 104, 108, 120, 133, 140

Spenser, Hugolin, 126

Stallen, 81

Stevens, Captain John, 19, 31, 32, 34, 35, 38, 41, 48, 51, 53, 60, 81, 87, 105, 113–14, 116, 118, 125, 126–7, 136–8, 143

Story, George Warter, 17, 18, 19, 36, 39, 41, 48, 49, 51, 52, 53, 54, 55, 56, 60, 61, 62, 63, 64, 65, 71, 83, 88, 89, 90, 91, 95, 97, 98, 99, 110, 116, 119, 131, 132, 139, 141

Sutherland, Colonel Hugh, 92; regiment of, 86, 91

Swords, 136, 137

Taafe, Father, 124

Tallanstown, 31, 48

Tanderagee, 33, 54

Tartaglia, Nicolo, 26

Tettau, Major-General Julius Ernst von, 96

Tirlon, Colonel, regiment of, 30, 80

Torbay, 8

Tourville, Admiral the Comte de, 44, 122, 147

Townley Hall, 59, 62, 76

Trant, Sir Patrick, 119

Trelawney, Brigadier Charles, 77, 139

Tuite, Brigadier William, 131

Tullyallen Hill, 59, 61, 62

Turenne, Henri de la Tour d'Auvergne, Vicomte de, 145

Tyrconnell, Richard Talbot, Duke of, 4, 5, 11–12, 13–14, 18, 29, 32, 36, 51, 57, 63, 71, 81, 85–8, 91, 95, 97, 102, 106, 107, 112, 120, 124, 125, 127, 130, 136, 143, 146, 147, 149, 150

Tyrconnell, Lady, 123

Villare Hibernicum (anon.), 20, 42, 50, 53, 61, 62, 84, 132, 136

Vindication of the True Account of the Siege of Londonderry (Walker), 99

Walker, George, bishop-elect of Derry, 23, 99

Walter, Hans Georg, 40, 96

Watts, William, 139

Wauchope, Major-General John, 81, 118, 125

Wexford, 137

Wharton, Thomas, 12

White, Sir Ignatius, 123

Whitehouse, Macedon Bay, 22, 32

William III: his army and equipment, 3–4, 17, 25–7, 35–6, 38, 42–6; accepts invitation to come to England, 7–8; lands at Torbay, 8; calls Convention Parliament, 9; declared King, 9; arrives in Belfast Lough, 15–16, 20–1; takes over command from Schomberg, 20, 42; in Belfast, 22–5, 32, 33; reviews troops, 32, 35, 39, 54; discusses strategy, 34–5; ill-health, 39–40, 70; marches on Dublin, 42, 46–8, 49, 55; coolness towards Schomberg, 42, 47, 68, 69, 70, 103; at Drogheda, 57, 59–61; tests troops' reaction to fire opposite Oldbridge, 60–5; wounds and narrow escapes, 63–5, 84, 104; council of war, 66–70; decides on feint from Slane and main attack at Oldbridge, 68–9; ability to encourage men, 70; forces way across river, 83–4, 88–110; leads Enniskilleners up hill of Donore, 107–8; his victory, 108–10, 120, 131–3; allows beaten army to escape, 115–16; concern for James, 115–16; losses, 131–2; encamps at Swords, 135, 137; at Finglas, 138, 139; triumphal entry into Dublin, 138–9; issues proclamation, 139–40; pressed to return to England, 141; at Limerick, 149; return to London, 149; effects of 'religious liberty' won by, 151–2

Wolseley, Colonel William, 36, 107; Enniskillen regiments of, 36, 43, 94, 107–8

Würtemberg-Neustadt, Lieutenant-General Ferdinand Wilhelm, Duke of, 22, 33, 40–1, 43, 48, 54, 61, 69, 93, 95–7, 98, 108, 120, 133, 138, 141

Yellow Island, 58, 59, 61, 62, 80, 93, 95, 97, 103, 132

Zurlauben, Conrad von, 116–17; Blue Regiment of, 27, 30, 46, 52, 80, 116–17, 138, 148